the
Weekend
Crafter®

Polymer Clay

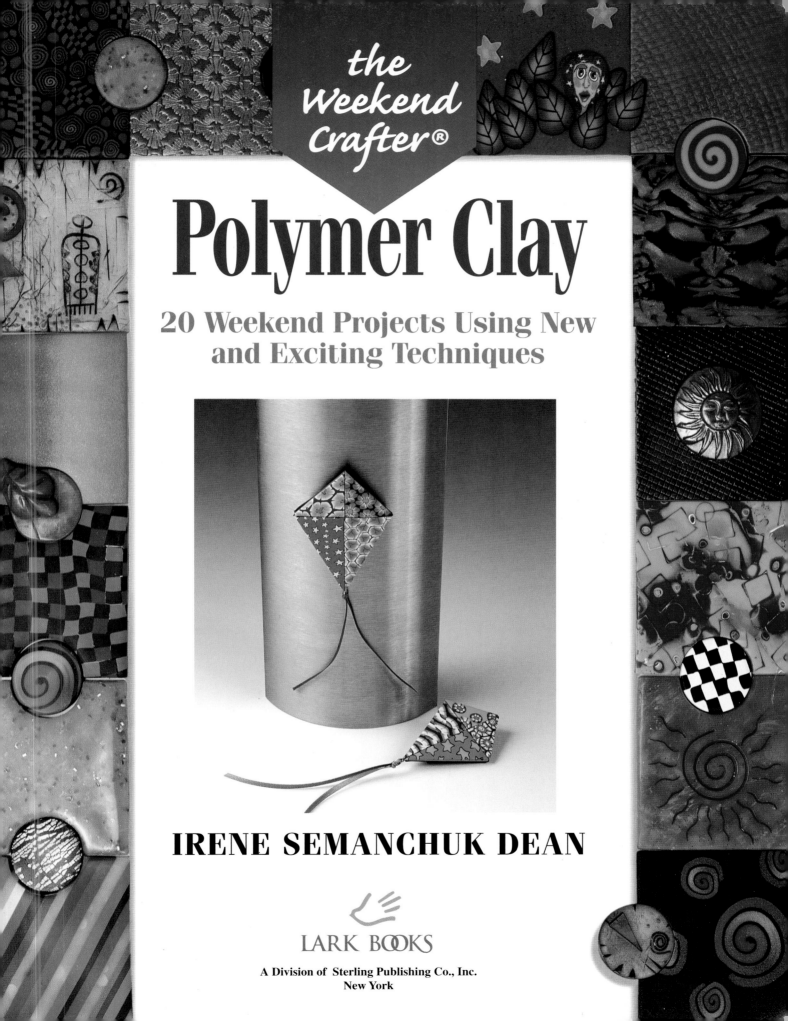

the Weekend Crafter®

Polymer Clay

20 Weekend Projects Using New and Exciting Techniques

IRENE SEMANCHUK DEAN

LARK BOOKS

A Division of Sterling Publishing Co., Inc.
New York

Editor: **Katherine M. Duncan**

Art Director: **Dana M. Irwin**

Photography: **Evan Bracken**

Editorial Assistance: **Heather Smith, Catharine Sutherland**

Production Assistance: **Hannes Charen**

Library of Congress Cataloging-in-Publication Data

Dean, Irene.

Polymer clay / Irene Dean.

p. cm. — (The weekend crafter)

Includes index.

ISBN 1-57990-168-9 (pbk.)

1. Polymer clay craft. I. Title. II. Series

TT297.D38 2000

731.4'2—dc21   00-025776

10 9 8 7 6 5 4 3

Published by Lark Books, a division of
Sterling Publishing Co., Inc.
387 Park Avenue South, New York, N.Y. 10016

© 2000, Irene Semanchuk Dean

Distributed in Canada by Sterling Publishing,
c/o Canadian Manda Group, One Atlantic Ave., Suite 105
Toronto, Ontario, Canada M6K 3E7

Distributed in the U.K. by:
Guild of Master Craftsman Publications Ltd.
Castle Place, 166 High Street, Lewes East Sussex, England BN7 1XU
Tel: (+ 44) 1273 477374, Fax: (+ 44) 1273 478606,
Email: pubs@thegmcgroup.com, Web: www.gmcpublications.com

Distributed in Australia by Capricorn Link (Australia) Pty Ltd., P.O. Box 704, Windsor, NSW 2756 Australia

If you have questions or comments about this book, please contact:
Lark Books, 50 College St., Asheville, NC 28801
(828) 253-0467
Manufactured in Hong Kong by Dai Nippon Printing Company
All rights reserved
ISBN 1-57990-168-9

Dedication

To Dad, I know you'd be proud.

Acknowledgments

A few thanks are in order. First, a world of thanks goes to Katherine Duncan, my editor, for guidance and encouragement in both the writing of the book and other areas—what began as a working relationship has turned into a friendship. And to Evan Bracken for his professional photography and helpful suggestions. Also, to Dana Irwin for doing a breathtaking job with the "glamour shots" in the book. And, lastly, to my husband Scott, for his patience, encouragement, and so much more.

Clock on page 1 by Irene Semanchuk Dean

INTRODUCTION

Irene Semanchuk Dean, *Java Quilt*, Polymer clay wall piece with canework and other techniques.

Polymer clay, a synthetic modeling material that is available in a wide range of colors, is one of the most exciting craft materials on the market today. An ideal medium for beginners and hobbyists, it produces beautiful results that don't require a lot of training or equipment.

Some of the simple techniques in this book will seem like magic when you first use them, and you'll get loads of instant gratification while learning them. Polymer clay is extremely compliant: you can easily fold it, texture it, stamp it, make it look like wood or stone, paint it, carve it, sand it, or drill it. It's easy to manipulate before it is baked, and won't dry out until it is baked to a durable, hardened state in a conventional oven. Its vibrant colors remain intact after baking, and it doesn't shrink or change shape during the baking process.

Despite its name, polymer clay isn't made of traditional clay, but a plastic called PVC (polyvinyl chlo-

ride) mixed with a plasticizer and color pigment. Polymer clay was introduced in Europe in the mid-20th century for dollmaking. Since then, artists and craftspeople have experimented with polymer clay and found it to be a perfect medium for building forms and decorating surfaces. Today you can buy a wide variety of polymer clays in craft and hobby stores, or order it by mail.

In comparison to other art forms, polymer clay is in its infancy. New techniques and uses are constantly being developed, and each new finding leads to others. The National Polymer Clay Guild was formed in 1990s, and regional guilds are springing up as the popularity of polymer clay grows. The Internet has also provided a way for polymer clay enthusiasts to share techniques and discoveries. As a result of its popularity among artists, spectacular works are now being created with this medium.

As a group, polymer clay users tend to generously share their ideas and discoveries. Perhaps this is a result of the newness of the material, or its accessibility to casual users. It's our hope that this book will encourage you to learn about and experiment with this fascinating, versatile medium.

A Personal Note

I first discovered polymer clay in 1992 when I was working at a local craft supply store. While I was there I learned to do such things as weave a rug, dye a shirt, marble paper, pour candles, and sew a pair of leather moccasins. But when I got my hands on polymer clay, I was home.

I loved the immediacy, versatility, and accessibility of it. I produced the first artwork of my life after discovering polymer clay. I began to sell what I made within six months of beginning, and, since 1997, I've been making and selling my work full-time. Like many people who first use this material, I started out making caneworked beads. Now I apply polymer clay in many other ways that range from beads to wall pieces.

Polymer clay is a great material for children and hobbyists—the immediacy of it is extremely satisfying, the colors are rich and intense, minimal tools and equipment are needed, and it is readily available in nearly all craft stores. Polymer clay has an infinite number of possibilities, many of which haven't even been pursued by artists yet. The field is wide open.

Such a forgiving medium seems to attract wonderful people. I have found the polymer clay community to be helpful and generous. We welcome new users and don't hesitate to answer technical questions and brainstorm. We often find one another on the internet where we share ideas, techniques, and projects with users all over the world.

I hope this book will be the beginning of your own enjoyment of this rich, exuberant medium.

Irene Semanchuk Dean, *Bird's Quilt*, Canework and handformed polymer clay. Collection of Kris Zipin and Roger Levy

The following section will chase away all your fears about polymer clay. You'll learn how to choose it, condition it, mix it, and bake it.

Brands

Several brands of polymer clay are available from which to choose. In general, different brands of clay have varying qualities, and each works well for certain types of projects. I'll point out a few observations below, but use your own judgement and develop your own preferences as you experiment with clays. There are a lot of great products on the market, and new ones are being developed all the time!

Most brands of polymer clay are sold in two-ounce (56 g) packages as well as larger, one-pound (.45 kg) bricks that can be special-ordered. Polyform Products creates several polymer clays including Sculpey III, which is a popular brand. Characteristically very soft and workable, it works well for children and beginners. After baking, it tends to be fragile, so I don't recommend it for projects that use thin sheets of clay. However, it works fine for solid shapes, and has a nice, slightly matte finish after it is baked.

Premo! Sculpey by Polyform Products was developed by Marie and Howard Segal of the Clay Factory of Escondido in response to a need for a polymer clay that combined the workability of Sculpey III with the strength and durability of Fimo polymer clay (see below). Premo is very easy to condition and work with, while being firm enough for creating distinct design elements. It is very strong and considerably flexible after baking.

Fimo, perhaps the best known brand among polymer clay users, is a product of Eberhard-Faber in Germany. Its firmness makes it an excellent clay for canework (see pages 21-24) because it ensures that intricate designs will remain distinct with little distortion. Fimo can be difficult to condition (see page 10), which is often frustrating for beginners. Because of this a polymer clay called Fimo Soft has been developed. Like Premo! Sculpey, Fimo Soft is easily conditioned, yet strong after baking.

Cernit polymer clay, a favorite of dollmakers because of its wide range of skin tone colors, is produced by the T+F GmbH Company in Germany. It has a medium-range texture that can be described as somewhere between the softness of Sculpey III and the firmness of Fimo. It will respond quickly to the heat of your hands, and, because of this, can be overworked easily. Cernit is strong and slightly flexible after it has been cured, and has a lovely, porcelain-like quality.

Other brands of polymer clay include Modelene (made in Australia) and Du-Kit (made in New Zealand). These clays are easily workable, without being too soft, and are extremely strong when baked. Jonco (a Dutch clay) and Formello (also called Modello) are both easily worked and are slightly less fragile than Sculpey III.

You can mix together any of the brands of polymer clay to create new colors or degrees of workability. If you do this, mix them thoroughly to achieve color consistency and strength. If they're not completely mixed, there may be weak areas in the resulting clay, especially if two dissimilar clays (such as Sculpey III and Fimo) are combined.

Color

Although polymer clay is available in a wide variety of colors, sometimes the package color is not quite the right shade for your design. Fortunately, you can mix polymer clays to create nearly any color. Many people mix colors randomly, adding a pinch of this and a smidgen of that until it's just right.

When creating your own color recipes, you should know some of the basics of mixing color that apply to paint and polymer clay. To darken a color, add small amounts of black. To lighten it, add some white. From the primary colors—red, yellow, and blue—you can make all other colors. Combine yellow and blue to get green, red and blue to get purple, and yellow and red to get orange. If you mix together complementary colors (red and green, yellow and purple, or orange and blue), you'll probably end up with brown, but a small pinch of each complementary color can create a nice effect.

In an overall design, choose colors that contrast in value as well as hue. If the colors are similar in value, you can separate them with "outlines" created by thin lines of black or another dark color, especially when working with canes that will be reduced to a smaller size.

If you think you may want to repeat a color that you've blended, write down the proportions of each of the colors that you combine. To make it simple to record proportions, use any size or shape of cutter to cut equal-sized pieces from sheets of various colors that you can then cut in half, quarters, or other parts of the whole before mixing. Using cutters enables you to create combinations on a small scale before you mix a larger batch of clay. Once you've established the color that you like and recorded the proportions, you can simply increase the quantities in the same proportion to one another to make a bigger batch.

After mixing the color, roll out a small, flat piece of it, and cut out a sample piece of it with a cutter. Punch a hole in the top with a drinking straw or other tool. Bake it, and after it cools, write the recipe directly on the clay with a permanent marker to create a color chip for future reference. As chips accumulate, string them on a cord or ball chain so that you'll always be able to find a color recipe for future projects.

Conditioning

Even though some brands of polymer clay feel soft and pliable right out of the package, they still need to be conditioned before being used. You can condition clay by hand through kneading, or run it through a pasta machine. Doing this thoroughly mixes the plasticizer throughout the clay, which makes it strong after baking. I can't overemphasize the importance of thoroughly conditioning any clay that you use.

Once you've conditioned your clay, it stays workable for awhile, but you should try to use conditioned clay within a month or so of kneading it. The plasticizer will settle in conditioned clay after a period of time, and you'll have to re-condition it before using it.

You may find it helpful to warm the clay slightly before conditioning it, especially if using a harder clay such as Fimo. I often put a wrapped package of clay in my pocket for awhile to warm it; or seal the clay in a plastic bag and leave it in a sink of warm water for 10 to15 minutes.

To condition polymer clay by hand, start with about an ounce (28 g) of a small block of clay. Roll it into a long snake, fold it a couple of times, and roll it back out. (Try not to incorporate air bubbles in the process of doing this.) Work it until it stretches and sags when you pull it apart, or for as long as it takes to mix two colors into one new color.

A pasta machine can make conditioning a breeze! Cut slabs from your block of clay that match the thickest setting on a pasta machine. Run each slab through, and add another on top before running both slabs through the machine. Fold the newly formed slab in half, and run it back through the machine. (Try not to trap air bubbles in the fold when you do this.) After about 20 folds and passes through the machine, your clay should be well conditioned; and, if combining two colors, they should be sufficiently mixed. Remember that once you've used your pasta machine for polymer clay, it can't be used for food again.

If your clay crumbles during conditioning, here are a few tricks that can help:

- Chop your obstinate clay into small pieces, and combine them with some small pieces of very soft clay in a plastic bag. After several days, the plasticizer from the soft clay will have leached into the harder clay, and you'll be able to mix these together thoroughly.

- Want results sooner? If you are willing to dedicate a food processor to your polymer clay obsession, you can use it to assist conditioning. Chop your clay into small pieces before putting them into the processor. (This is another great opportunity to create custom color mixes.) Run the processor in short bursts. If the blade is jamming, chop up the larger pieces of clay. Keep a close eye on what's happening in the processor while doing this. The clay will get chopped into very tiny bits, and then the action and the heat will make these bits start to clump up. Stop just as this begins to happen. Remove the clay from the bowl, and place it on your work surface. Flatten it with your brayer or the heel of your hand. After this step, condition by hand or with your pasta machine.

- Conditioning can be aided by products on the market made specifically for this purpose. These products come in block form or liquid form and are available in stores that sell polymer clay.

If your polymer clay is too sticky and soft, you can remove some of the excess plasticizer by leaching it. To do this, flatten the squishy clay into a sheet, and place it between two pieces of paper before weighing it down with a few heavy books. Let it sit overnight. The next day you'll find an oily film on the paper, which is the plasticizer that's been leached out. The clay may be fine at this point, but if it isn't, leach it some more until it reaches the perfect consistency. Recondition your clay after this process.

Storing

Keep your packages of polymer clay away from direct sunlight and heat. You can store your clay in plastic food bags or plastic lidded containers. Since polymer clay reacts to some kinds of hard plastic, it's a good idea to store the clay in its original plastic packaging or wrap it in wax paper before putting it into a plastic container. I prefer to store clay in slabs folded between pieces of wax paper because they are easier to run through the pasta machine for conditioning.

If you're storing canes that you've made, make sure that they're not exposed to heat, sunlight, dust, or pet hair. Wrap each cane in wax paper or plastic wrap, or keep them in a plastic box lined with wax paper. Storage containers with compartments and drawers can come in handy for this purpose.

Baking

Since most polymer clays cure at a low temperature of around 275° F (135° C), you can use your own oven for baking projects. If you use the same oven for baking food and polymer clay, I advise that you allow the oven to cool, and wipe the inside with baking soda and water before using it for food again. If you intend to bake polymer clay on a regular basis, invest in a dedicated oven—an inexpensive toaster oven will work well enough for hobby purposes. Be aware that toaster ovens tend to cycle on and off, resulting in temperature spikes that may burn the clay. To prevent this, place a tent of aluminum foil over your baking tray while curing the clay. Be aware of heating elements above and below the baking area in a toaster oven that might scorch your clay. If you're making a lot of polymer clay work, a convection oven provides a larger space for baking, and the temperature is more consistent.

Always use an oven thermometer to make sure the temperature is accurate in any oven that you use. Baking at a temperature that is too low will result in weak, fragile pieces, and an oven that is too hot will burn your pieces, especially the lighter colored ones. Since polymer clay lets off fumes when you bake it, always ventilate the room in which you're baking by turning on a fan and opening the windows. This is especially important if you (oops!) burn a project.

The jury is still out on the necessity of preheating your oven when baking polymer clay. As long as the clay bakes for the proper amount of time at the right temperature, it doesn't seem to matter whether the oven was preheated or not. After baking, it seems that allowing polymer clay to cool slowly in the oven makes for a stronger finished piece. After the piece has baked for its appropriate time, turn the oven off and crack the door to cool it without a sudden temperature change.

Polymer clay doesn't shrink when baked, but some objects will need to be supported during baking to keep them from sagging. Bake beads on a skewer or in a shallow trough made of a folded piece of paper, and odd-shaped objects on a nest of polyester fiberfill or gently wadded cotton cloth.

If you bake on a glass or metal tray, your piece will be shiny where it came in contact with the tray. I use manila folders cut to the size of my baking tray to prevent these shiny spots. You can also use mat board scraps from a picture framer for this purpose. Be sure to place your object on the untextured side of mat board.

Polymer clay can be rebaked many times, and you'll find instances where this will be needed. Be sure that the entire piece is baked for an adequate amount of time, even if a large portion of it has already been baked.

Common Sense Safety Tips

Exercise common sense when using polymer clay.

■ Polymer clay is a synthetic substance, so be careful that a child or pet doesn't swallow it.

■ Don't snack while you are working with clay. Not only will you get cracker crumbs in your project, but you might accidentally ingest small amounts of the clay.

■ Tools that you use for polymer clay should never be used for food, so dedicate your pasta machine or canapé cutters to your craft work.

■ Ventilate well when baking polymer clay—don't breathe the fumes! If you burn the clay, open the windows immediately, and turn on a fan.

■ If you plan to bake more than an occasional piece, you might wish to purchase a small toaster oven or even a convection oven to use exclusively for polymer clay. If you use your home oven, clean it inside with baking soda and water after baking to remove any residue.

■ Before you rub your eyes, bathe the baby, or make dinner, wash your hands thoroughly after working with polymer clay. Before washing, I like to rub hand lotion into my palms and fingers before rubbing it off with a terrycloth rag. Then I wash with soap and cold water and a nailbrush to remove all traces of clay from under my fingernails. (The lotion seems to break down the clay a bit and make it easier to remove; cold water makes any remaining clay a little stiffer and easier to remove with the nailbrush.)

■ Polymer clay pieces should never be used for drinking or eating, or as ashtrays.

TOOLS AND TRICKS

Most of the tools that you'll use for rolling, cutting, shaping, and embellishing polymer clay are common things that have been adapted to these uses. Take a peek inside the toolbox of someone who works with polymer clay, and you're likely to see an odd assortment of things such as a rolling pin, golf tee, wallpaper scraper, or dental pick.

Preparing and Rolling Out the Clay

First, you'll need a work surface that is appropriate for rolling and cutting clay. Preferences for work surfaces vary as widely as the people who use them. I am fortunate to use my late grandmother's white enameled table that was used for making *pierogi*. The metal surface cleans easily and stays cool in the summer. A large sheet of beveled glass works well as a work surface. If the edges of the glass are unbeveled, protect yourself from cuts by covering them with masking tape. If you're working on glass, you can slide a pattern or grid underneath it to guide you in cutting the clay. White ceramic tiles from a home improvement store also work well, and allow you to move the project from one surface to another or set it aside intact. These tiles can also be put directly into the oven. Both glass and tile won't be marred by the use of blades. Use rubbing alcohol or baby oil to clean your work surface and tools between steps.

Besides your hands, the most necessary polymer clay tools are a rolling pin or pasta machine for making slabs of clay, and a blade for cutting it. You'll begin nearly all of the projects in this book by rolling the polymer clay into slabs or sheets. If you're just beginning, and don't want to invest in a pasta machine for rolling out the clay, you can use a rolling pin or any smooth-surfaced cylindrical tool. Old-fashioned wooden rolling pins will leave grain marks in the clay and eventually become sticky, so try to find a smooth-surfaced one made of acrylic or plastic. Black rubber or clear acrylic printers' brayers from craft supply stores also work well for smoothing the clay, as do solid or hollow acrylic rods.

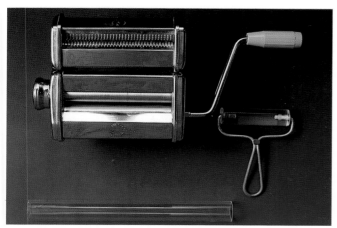

A pasta machine, an acrylic brayer, and a hollow lucite roller are all accessible tools that can be used to roll out polymer clay.

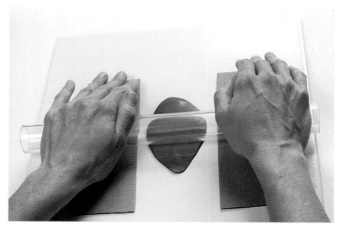

Using a lucite roller to roll out a sheet of polymer clay

If you're rolling the clay by hand, select two dowels that are of the width that you want for your clay sheet. Place a dowel on either side of the clay underneath the roller. As you flatten the clay with the roller, it will get trapped between the dowels on either side of it and reach a uniform thickness. To roll thinner sheets, use narrow skewers or sheets of cardboard instead of the dowels.

If you find that you are getting addicted to polymer clay, the purchase of a pasta machine will make your life much easier. A pasta machine is ideal for rolling clay into uniform, thin sheets. (You won't be able to roll out paper-thin sheets by hand.) Since forcing a thick wad of polymer clay through the machine's rollers can bend the scrapers and damage the machine, you should flatten the clay first with your hands or a roller before feeding it through the machine. If you're aiming for a paper-thin sheet, feed the clay through the machine several times at progressively thinner settings to create a progressively thinner sheet, rather than trying to crank thicker clay through a very narrow setting on the machine. You can also purchase a motor to fit the pasta machine, which leaves both hands free while you manipulate the clay.

Cutting and Sculpting the Clay

After you've rolled out the clay, you'll most likely be cutting it. Some people prefer craft knives for cutting the clay; others like to use surgical tissue blades. Craft knives have a handle that makes them safer to use, but somewhat awkward for clay. Surgical tissue blades are extremely thin and sharp, but sometimes flex too much. I prefer to use a wallpaper blade or paint scraper from a paint store because they are flexible but stiffer than tissue blades. These blades are double-sided, so be careful when using them! For children, try a pottery cutting rib from a craft supply store. (Even these have sharp edges, so always supervise children when they're using them.)

The blade that you choose to use is often dictated by the type of cut you need to make. A craft knife is suitable for cutting tight curves and angles, carving intricate detail, or making a cut that is longer than your cutting blade. You'll need a cutting blade for making a smooth, clean cut without dragging the blade

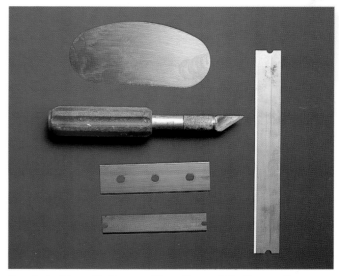

Top to bottom: Pottery cutting rib, craft knife, wallpaper scraper blade, paint scraper blade

through the clay, such as when you're cutting out a distinct shape to make into a piece of jewelry or cutting mokume gane slices.

Cookie cutters, canapé cutters, and clay cutters made for ceramics are handy to cut out specific shapes such as hearts, stars, or circles. Cut several of the same shape from a sheet of polymer clay, roll each into a ball, and you'll be able to make beads of a uniform size.

A V-shaped gouge called a veiner that is used by printmakers for cutting linoleum blocks works wonderfully for carving designs and patterns in polymer clay. After the designs are carved, another color of clay can be used to fill in or grout the gouged areas. The excess clay is then wiped from the surface, and the piece is baked again. The carving can also be enhanced by rubbing acrylic paint into the grooves and wiping the excess from the surface.

Sculpting tools found in the pottery or ceramics section of a craft supply store, or everyday objects such as golf tees, dental tools, crochet hooks, toothpicks, and cuticle shapers are helpful for sculpting, finishing, and embossing the clay on your project.

If you are planning a clay sculpture, consider using an armature to add strength and bulk to the otherwise fragile elements of a piece. Stiff twisted wire can be shaped, then covered with polymer clay to make such features as arms, tails, or legs. Cover a tightly wadded shape of aluminum foil instead of building something from solid polymer clay, and you'll save both time and money. Be certain that your armature is able to withstand the temperature for baking polymer clay, and that there are no air bubbles or pockets where the clay and the armature meet.

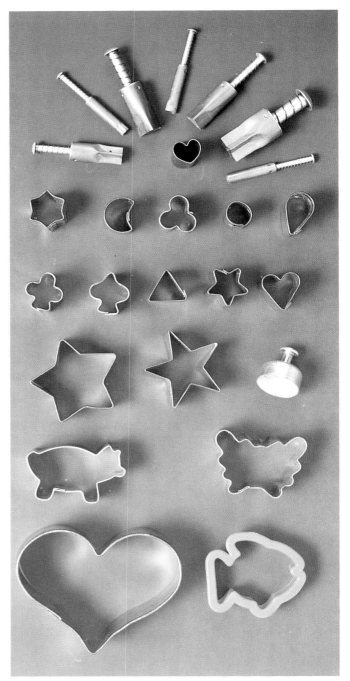

Cutters that come in a variety of shapes and sizes can be used for making flat shapes from polymer clay.

Making Beads

For making beads, you'll need a tool to make holes through them before baking them. A needle tool, which is a pottery tool, works perfectly for this purpose. (You can also make your own needle tool by embedding a needle into a wad of clay and baking it.) Other options include skewers that you'll find in grocery stores, steel weaving needles or quilting pins from craft stores or yarn shops, and metal knitting needles for making larger holes to accommodate thicker stringing material.

When you use one of these tools, make certain to pierce your bead from both sides to avoid a messy exit

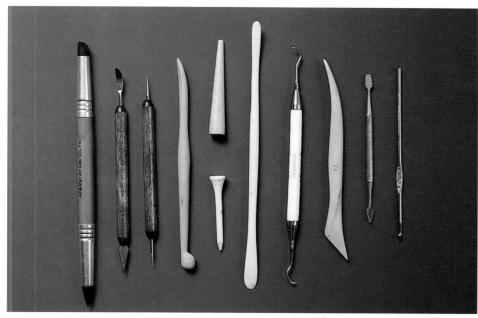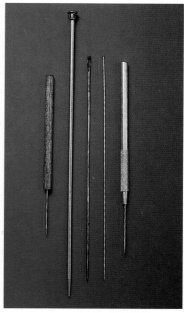

Left: Many everyday items can be used to sculpt polymer clay. (Left to right: Paint pusher, pottery tool, ball-ended tool, sculpting tool, chair caning peg, golf tee, sculpting tool, dental tool, sculpting tool, cuticle shaper, crochet hook) Right: Any long and thin tool with a sharp point can be used to pierce beads. (Left to right: Needle tool, knitting needle, weaving needle, long hat pin, needle tool)

Clay gun with discs

hole. Leave your beads on the tool for baking, cut grooves in the sides of a shallow box, and rest the tool with beads across them so that they won't become distorted during baking. If you're using quilting pins, you can stick the pins into an upside-down aluminum foil pie pan for baking.

Sometimes it is not feasible to pierce a hole in a piece before baking because it might distort an essential part of the design. Holes can be drilled after baking with a hand-held electric mini-drill tool or by hand with a pin vise (a tiny hand drill available from a railroad hobby store).

A clay gun can come in handy for extruding lengths of clay to be used for decorative borders or cut beads. A variety of templates come with the tool, which allow you to create differently shaped pieces of clay.

Adding Texture to the Clay

Add texture to polymer clay with a variety of objects such as leather, sandpaper, lace, textured fabric, rubber stamps, window screen, plastic embroidery canvas, old costume jewelry, coins, keys, seashells, or tree bark. When you begin your search for texture, your eyes will become accustomed to seeking out interesting surfaces, and it can become an obsession. Those who love you most will soon offer you something precious that they've found, such as a piece of a broken car taillight or a rubber toy alligator because they know you'll like its texture.

Use a release agent of some sort between the texturing materials and the clay, or the clay will end up sticking to them. You can simply apply water to the clay with a quick spritz from a spray bottle for this purpose; or brush cornstarch onto the clay or object with a soft make-up brush, and blow off the excess. Use mica powders for a release agent if you want to add sparkle and color to your piece, and protect them with a finish so that they don't flake off (see page 17). Talcum powder and metallic powders also work well, but these can be harmful to breathe, so wear a dust mask when using them.

SURFACE FINISHES

A variety of surface finishes can be used on polymer clay. Shimmering metallic color can be added to the surface of polymer clay with mica-based powders, which come in a variety of colors. (Although it's never a good idea to inhale any foreign substance, mica-based powders are potentially less harmful than metal-based powders.) You can apply powders with a small, dry paintbrush, a fingertip, or a rubber stamp. Seal and protect the powder from rubbing off with a coat of varnish (see page 19), or mix them into varnish or liquid polymer clay (see page 18) before painting them on the clay. There are several brands of powders available on the market. The type of powder that you choose will depend on the project that you're making and your personal preferences.

You can also embellish the surface of your polymer clay with ultra-thin metal leaf, often referred to as gold or silver leaf. Real silver and gold leaf are expensive, so I often use aluminum and bronze leaf. Some art and craft supply stores also carry a metal leaf variegated with bronze and copper color. Because it is fragile and will stick to your fingers easily, you should place the clay on top of the leaf rather than the other way around. Metal leaf has to be protected so that it doesn't flake off of your piece. You can accomplish this by either applying a very thin layer of translucent clay before baking it, or a coat of varnish after baking.

A variety of materials can be used to impart texture to polymer clay.

While there are some tools that have been created just for polymer clay, many of the tools that you'll find useful have origins elsewhere. Tools are very personal, and you'll find yourself reaching for that golf tee or cookie cutter over and over again. Adapt your own finds to polymer clay, and soon you'll be sharing your own information with others!

Along with metal leaf, you can apply anything to polymer clay that can withstand baking at a low temperature. Create interesting collages by adding such elements as postage stamps, twigs, fabric, or metal charms to the surface.

Mica powders come in a multitude of colors.

After it has been baked, you can paint polymer clay with acrylic paints or draw on it with colored pencils. A light-colored clay with a matte surface will yield the best results for colored pencil drawings. Before baking the clay that you intend to color with pencils, lightly press 800-grit sandpaper into it to give the surface a tooth. Protect the colored surface with a coat of varnish; or apply an ultra-thin layer of translucent clay or liquid polymer clay (see page 18), and bake it again.

INCLUSIONS

Inclusions are things that are mixed into the polymer clay to change the appearance of the clay. Glitter, mica powders, crayon shavings, bits of mylar, colored sand, and spices all make interesting inclusions, especially in translucent polymer clay. Any substances that you add to the clay can change when you heat them, so experiment with any new inclusions in some scrap clay, and bake it before using them in a final piece. Because clay with inclusions can eventually dull your cutting blade, it's a good idea to dedicate one of your blades to this clay.

Mica powders may be mixed directly into the polymer clay to change the appearance of the clay. Larger-grained powders work especially well for this purpose. Embossing powders, which are often used for rubber stamping, also make interesting inclusions. Many of them pop slightly when heated, resulting in a piece that looks a little different from what you put in the oven.

If you choose to use glitter, remember that some glitters are made of plastic and others of metal. Some plastic glitters can't withstand baking, so make sure to experiment with them before making a final piece.

Keep in mind that adding inclusions to the polymer clay tends to weaken it, since these added substances change its structure. Experiment with your chosen inclusions embedded in scrap clay to arrive at the right proportion for the effect you want without compromising the strength of your finished piece.

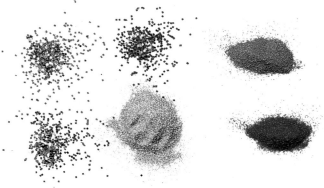

ADDING AND TAKING AWAY

The following section covers the specifics of gluing, varnishing, sanding, and buffing polymer clay after you've baked it.

Glues

Several glues work well for different polymer clay uses. Most white glues are made of PVA (polyvinyl acetate), a substance which is related to polymer clay. Among the white glues, a brand named Sobo is among the best to use because it is heat and UV resistant. It is often used to cover wooden armatures before adding polymer clay to them, since clay won't stick to wood. For ease in handling, allow heat-resistant PVA glue to dry completely before applying polymer clay to it.

In the projects that follow, you'll use glue to attach pin backs, earring backs, barrette backs, and magnets to polymer clay pieces. Before you do this, make certain that you clean the baked polymer clay and the object that you're attaching with a cotton ball and rubbing alcohol before gluing them together. (New jewelry findings and other metal objects often have a very fine coating of oil on them, that is left over from the machining process. Wiping the polymer piece eliminates any residue that might interfere with the gluing process.)

Choose a glue that works well for your purposes. For instance, E6000 is a glue that is very appropriate for hair barrettes because of its flexibility. Cyanoacrylate glues, like Superglue or Zap-A-Gap, are also highly compatible with polymer clay. Ventilate well when you're using any of these glues.

Liquid Polymer Clay

Liquid polymer clay (such as Liquid Sculpey) can be used for a variety of uses. (Check the sources listing in the back of this book on page 80 for mail order sources.) This product works better than any glue for adhering baked or unbaked pieces of polymer clay to others. Since it is made of the same substance as polymer clay, a superior bond is created. Keep in mind that you'll need to bake it after you've applied it, even if you're using it to attach already-baked pieces to one another.

You can also tint liquid polymer with oil paints or mica powders, and brush it onto the clay surface as a colored wash. A thin coat of liquid polymer can be applied, baked, sanded, and buffed to create a glossy, transparent finish that is similar to varnish.

Liquid polymer clay works incredibly well for transferring images to polymer clay. Brush a thin coating onto a sheet of clay, press the photocopied image onto the surface, and you'll be amazed at the results (see page 26 for more information on transfers).

Leftover amounts of this product can be stored in a paper cup covered with plastic wrap for several days. Store it in a small glass jar for longer periods. If it needs to be thinned out, use a liquid conditioner. This product should be baked at a minimum of 275° F (135° C) for 10 minutes. Some people find it bakes harder and clearer when the baking temperature is bumped to 300°F (149° C) for a few minutes. Use caution when baking because it creates fumes, and the fumes increase with the temperature.

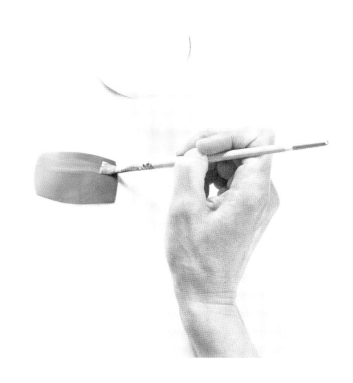

Varnishes

Unvarnished polymer clay has its own lovely finish; but, if you prefer a shinier surface, you may want to varnish your baked piece. Varnish is essential if you need to protect powder, metallic leaf, colored pencil, or other surface finishes from flaking or rubbing off.

Polymer clay manufacturers (such as Eberhard Faber and Polyform Products) produce varnishes for polymer clay. Varnishes made for other purposes may or may not work. Some are compatible with clay, and others aren't, so experiment with brands before you make your choice.

Clear nail polish is not a good varnish for polymer clay, nor are most of the spray varnishes that are available. (One spray varnish brand that has been used successfully on polymer clay is Artworks Matte Spray Varnish.) Although these finishes will appear dry, the piece will be sticky within a few weeks or months.

Sanding and Buffing

You can achieve a beautiful shine without varnish by sanding and buffing your piece. To keep yourself from inhaling harmful dust, always use wet/dry sandpaper that has been dipped in water to sand the baked clay. The water will also serve to keep the piece cool, and prevent the sandpaper from leaving marks caused by the heating action of sanding.

Remember that the smoother you make your piece in raw clay, the easier it will be to sand later. Make sure that your piece has cooled completely before sanding it. Start sanding with rough sandpaper (400-grit works well) to remove any fingerprints and unwanted bumps. Watch what you're doing; you don't want to accidentally sand away parts of your design. Some people prefer to sand in alternating directions with each grit—for instance, up and down with 400-grit, side to side with 600-grit, and up and down with 800-grit. Others like to sand in a circular motion. You'll find a style and rhythm that feels most comfortable to you. Wet your sandpaper regularly to rinse off the accumulating polymer clay debris.

Work up to the shine that you desire by moving from 400-grit to 600-grit to 800-grit without skipping grits. The higher the grit number, the finer the sandpaper. (Very finely graded sandpaper is available at auto parts stores.) After you've worked your way up to at least 800-grit, you may wish to stop and leave the piece as is, or buff it on a piece of soft denim or a cotton muslin buffing wheel. If you choose to invest in a buffing wheel, you can purchase a jeweler's buffing wheel, available from a jewelry supply store or catalog, or you can use a bench grinder with a cotton wheel in place of the stone one from a home improvement store.

Practice caution when buffing! The wheel moves at an extremely high speed. Before you even turn the motor on, tie back any long hair, and remove necklaces or dangling bracelets. It is also advisable to wear eye protection and a dust mask, since tiny bits of cotton fiber from the wheel become airborne while buffing. Always hold your polymer clay piece next to the underside of the wheel when buffing—if it gets snatched from your fingertips (and this happens more often than you might think), it will shoot away from you instead of towards you. Make certain that there are no children, pets, windows, or fragile things in the line of fire. Keep your piece moving constantly—holding it in one place will result in friction that can begin to melt the clay.

Buffing takes some practice, but the results can be breathtaking, especially when using translucent or metallic clays.

TECHNIQUES

From the simplest to the most complex technique, the following basics will fill you in on how to transform a lump of clay into a work of art.

Marbling Color

Probably the first thing we instinctually do with polymer clay is to squish and mash a handful of different colors together until a lovely swirled effect appears. Knowing when to stop is perhaps the most important part of marbling two or more colors together. Make sure your colors are all conditioned and of approximately the same consistency before making a serious attempt at marbling.

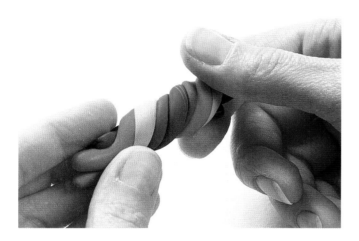

There are endless things that you can do with marbled clay. Once you've swirled together your colors and are happy with the effect, you can roll the clay into a tube, and slice it into individual pieces for beads. These can be used as focal beads in a finished piece, or they can become pleasing spacer beads used between larger, more elaborate beads. You can also roll out the marbled clay into a sheet, and use it as a background for embellishment, or cut it into shapes to use in any way that you please.

Canework

You're probably already familiar with canework, the most well-known use of polymer clay that is often used to make jewelry. Originally known in glasswork as *millefiori* ("a thousand flowers"), canework originated in Venice and was adopted by polymer clay users. Intricate and intriguing patterned slices can be used to make beads, or cover objects with a dazzling surface. There are many books on the market that give detailed instructions about canework. We've covered the basics below, and used canework in a few of the projects to follow. If you don't want to make your own canes, you can purchase pre-made canes. But, of course, they won't have your own creative stamp on them.

Making a cane from polymer clay is a considerably easier task than making one in glass. When using polymer clay, you won't be limited to making canes with rod shapes as you would if using glass. You can make canes from elongated triangles, squares, or sheets of varied sizes and thicknesses that can be arranged in a log to form a pattern or image that is revealed when the cane is sliced. (Think of a jellyroll cake in which the spiral of jelly runs through the entire cake, and each slice has the same pattern.) Depending on its size, a cane may yield dozens or hundreds of slices.

Clays that you combine into one cane should be of the same consistency. (A simple way to make certain that this happens is to use the same brand of clay throughout the cane.) If, for example, you mix a very soft clay with a firm clay, the softer clay will reduce faster and squish out when you reduce the cane, and you'll end up with a distorted image. Use colors that contrast in hue and value, so that your reduced design is discernable. Separate similar colors in your cane with a sheet of black or white clay to define them.

After building a cane, allow it to rest before reducing it, preferably overnight. Doing this lessens the chance of distortion, because it gives all the components of the cane a chance to cool to the same temperature. After resting, use your hands to reduce the cane to a smaller diameter with careful and deliberate squeezing, pressing, and rolling. To begin elongating the cane, squeeze the sides gently with a fisted hand, or leave it on your work surface and press it with the heel of your hand. Then slowly and gently roll it back and forth with deliberate motions to lengthen the cane and reduce it in diameter. To minimize distortion, make sure you reduce the cane evenly from one end to the other (if the cane is too long to handle, cut off sections small enough to roll evenly). Repeat this process until you have several diameters of the same cane. If you handle the clay carefully, the design or image will remain intact.

To reduce a square cane, use your rolling pin or brayer to roll from the center of the cane to each end. Continue this process, and occasionally flip it over so that the direction of the pressure you're applying is even on both ends.

After reducing a cane, it will be warmed up from rolling and squeezing, and may distort when you slice it. For this reason, you should allow it to rest overnight before slicing it with a clean, sharp blade. (To prevent smears, clean your blade with rubbing alcohol or a baby wipe cloth after each slice.) Rotate the cane a quarter turn before making your next slice, so that you are not applying pressure to the same side, which could result in a distorted edge. If your slices are smeared, your cane may be too warm, so allow it to rest. If it's warm in your work area, set the cane in the refrigerator until it's cool enough to slice cleanly.

To keep a round cane from getting a flat bottom when you slice it, make a trough to fit the cane from scrap clay. Mash together scrap clay in an elogated form, and then press a roller or a fat marker into the clay to make a long indentation. Position the round cane in the trough, and slice through the whole thing with your cutting blade.

Use the canework slices as a surface decoration on base beads, background slabs, or objects such as glass candle holders. Place them close together on the surface that you're decorating, then roll them with a brayer to diminish the seams between them. Save a slice from every cane that you make as a record of what does (and doesn't) work.

Canework Patterns

In the following section you'll find simple instructions for several basic canes that can be used as the basis for creating more complex designs and patterns. No specific thicknesses or sizes are suggested—you'll soon discover how differently sized elements will create different effects. Experiment and have fun!

HOW TO MAKE A JELLYROLL CANE

Use a rolling pin or pasta machine to roll out two or more rectangular sheets of different colors of clay. Stack the sheets, gently press them together to eliminate air bubbles, and trim the edges so that they're all the same size. Turn one of the short ends of the stack upwards, and roll up the stack to form a tube.

HOW TO MAKE A BULL'S-EYE CANE

Use your hands to roll out a single color of clay into a snake-like tube that is the length of the cane you want to make. Use a rolling pin or pasta machine to roll out a sheet of a contrasting clay, and cut it to a width that is as wide as the tube is long. Make a clean, straight cut along the leading edge of the sheet, and press the tube gently into place along this edge. Carefully roll up the tube inside the sheet. Where the leading edge presses into the sheet on the work surface, slice away the excess clay, and butt the two edges together. Repeat this process to add as many rings as you like.

HOW TO MAKE A LACE CANE

This is a variation of the bull's-eye cane that works well if you alternate black and white clay. Wrap a narrow, snake-like tube in a contrasting sheet of clay, then reduce it until it is at least 6 inches (15 cm) long. Cut the tube into four or more equal lengths, then bundle and compress them until they adhere to each other. Reduce this bundle until it is long enough to cut into several more equal lengths to bundle together into a new configuration. Repeat this process until the desired effect is achieved.

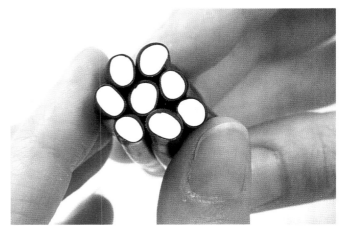

HOW TO MAKE A CANE WITH A COOKIE CUTTER

Use a cookie cutter to make a cane that has a star, heart, or other design embedded in the center. To do this, condition at least an ounce (28 g) each of two contrasting colors of clay, and form each into a slightly flattened circle on your work surface. Apply a water or cornstarch as a mold release to the inside and outside of the cookie cutter, and cut out shapes from the center of each wad of clay. Remove the shapes from each section of clay, and switch each to the other clay. (You'll end up with two cane possibilities by doing this.) Gently compress the outside clay to eliminate air pockets before reducing the cane.

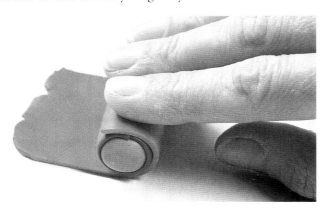

HOW TO MAKE A STRIPED CANE

Stack together two or more sheets of clay in contrasting colors. Cut the stack in half, and place one half on top of the other. Repeat this process until you've achieved the number of stripes that you want. If needed, reduce the stack by rolling it with a brayer.

HOW TO MAKE A SIMPLE FLOWER CANE

Make a bull's-eye cane with several rings of different colors that graduate in thickness as you move outward. Roll gently to compress them without reducing them. Use a blunt-edged tool, such as a straightedge, credit card, or the dull side of a cutting blade, to press an indentation halfway into the cane along the length of the cane. Add other indentations around the circumference of the cane to create as many petals as you like.

HOW TO MAKE A CHECKERBOARD CANE

Use a rolling pin or pasta machine to roll two sheets of contrasting colors of clay to the same thickness. Press them together gently, and trim them so that the edges are even. Cut this slab into strips, and flip over every other strip to create alternating strips. Cut this slab in half crosswise. Stack one section on top of the other to create a checkerboard pattern.

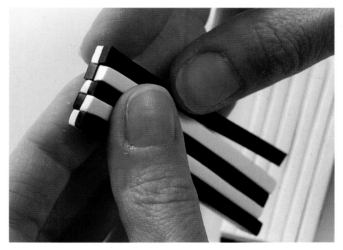

CANES GONE WRONG

We've all made 'em. After planning, conditioning, rolling, stacking, compressing, and reducing you end up with a lopsided teapot, a sad looking flower, or a mouse with no ears.

There are a couple of caning alternatives for your mishaps. Try cutting them into pieces lengthwise, and reassemble the pieces differently to make abstract patterned canes. Another alternative is to make the distorted cane the center of a bull's eye, and wrap it in one or more sheets of contrasting color before reducing, cutting, and reassembling it into a lace cane.

If all else fails, you'll have some scrap clay for making molds or for use as base beads to be covered in mille-fiori slices.

How to Make a Skinner Blend

Many rather ordinary designs can be transformed into sophisticated work with the use of Skinner blends. This unique method of creating polymer clay that transitions smoothly from one color to another is attributed to polymer clay artist Judith Skinner.

You'll need a pasta machine to create a Skinner blend. Select two or more colors of polymer clay that you'd like to blend together, and condition the clay before beginning. Use the pasta machine to roll each color out into a sheet, and cut each color into a triangle. Position

the triangles as shown, alternating the colors. Gently press the seams together. Run this new sheet through the pasta machine, then fold it in half from bottom to top, and run it through the machine again. (It is vital that you fold the clay in the same direction every time. If you fold it incorrectly even once, it will destroy the effect.) Repeat the folding and blending process 20 to 30 times, until each color fades subtly into the next.

You can alter the shape of the triangles, or make the edges curved to create different blends. When you're deciding what colors to blend, think about the color that will result.

Once you've blended the clay, you can use it in sheet form, or as an element in a cane. To make a shaded bull's-eye cane from Skinner blend, turn the blended sheet 90 degrees, and pass it through the pasta machine on progressively thinner settings until you have reached the thinnest sheet that you can handle. Trim one of the short edges, and roll it up from that edge as tightly and evenly as possible. This interesting cane can then be used as a component in a variety of complex canes.

Mokume Gane

Mokume gane (moe-KOO-may GAH-nay) is a Japanese metalworking technique that has been adapted to polymer clay. Polymer clay mokume gane is a little less time-consuming and strenuous than metalworking, and you can produce a stunning, organic-looking surface embellishment by stacking and slicing sheets of clay. There are countless variations in the combinations you can choose that will give different effects. In addition to regular opaque clays, you can use tinted translucents, metal leaf between polymer clay sheets, or any combination of these for mokume gane.

To create mokume gane slices, use a pasta machine to roll two or more colors of clay into thin sheets. Make a stack from several sheets. To cut slices with wide rings and simple, pleasing patterns, flex your cutting blade slightly before carving out divots and channels. For a variation, apply small balls of coordinating colors of polymer clay to one side of the stack, flip it over, and press the stack into the balls to create a bumpy surface on top before slicing. You can also create complex patterns by making indentations with a variety of objects in the stacked clay before slicing it, as shown below.

The mokume gane slices can be applied to any polymer clay surface as decoration. (The pattern will be different on each side of each slice, so check to see which you prefer.) Roll small slices onto a polymer bead, or arrange them on a sheet of clay, and flatten them with your brayer before cutting the sheet into the shape that you need.

Faux Natural Materials

You can imitate a wide range of natural materials such as turquoise, malachite, granite, opal, amber, and wood by adding inclusions to polymer clay, treating the surface with indentations and color, or layering certain colors. Faux stone benefits from thorough sanding and buffing to create a deep shine. Acrylic paint enhances the texture of faux wood or slate.

Assortment of polymer clay artifacts by Luann Udell

Molds

Making a mold from polymer clay can allow you to duplicate an object of your choice to make a series of items such as buttons, earrings, or beads.

Begin with a wad of scrap clay large enough to take the impression of your object. Apply a mold release (water or cornstarch), and press the object into the clay. Remove it and check to see that the impression is good, then bake the clay for about 30 minutes. Once the mold has cooled completely, dust or spray it with a mold release. Form a piece of clay 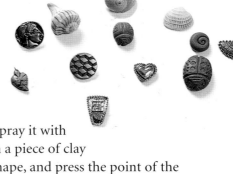 into a stubby cone shape, and press the point of the cone into the center of the mold. Continue to press the entire piece of raw clay into the mold until you have filled the cavity completely. Slice off any excess that isn't needed on the back, and gently pull the clay from the mold.

Transfers

Photo transfers are extremely popular for all sorts of crafts, and polymer clay is no exception. It's a rewarding process that you can do in a few simple steps.

First, choose the image that you want to apply to your clay, and make a photocopy of it. Here are a few tips to remember:

- The transferred image will be a mirror image of the original.
- The toner used in copiers is what will transfer to the clay; inkjet printer ink will not transfer.
- A machine with fresh toner is more likely to produce better results.
- A recently made photocopy will yield better transfer results than an old one.

Soon after copying your image, lay the photocopy inkside down onto a sheet of light-colored clay. Burnish the paper with the back of a spoon or other burnishing tool. Allow the clay to sit for 15 to 20 minutes, and then bake it for 15 minutes at the clay manufacturer's recommended temperature. While the clay is still warm, remove the paper to reveal your transferred image. Photocopy transfers are permanent on polymer clay, so varnishing isn't necessary, unless you want to add gloss to your image.

Drawings done in colored pencil also make good transfers. To transfer a drawing, follow the same procedure as for a photocopy transfer. The more intensely colored your drawing is, the brighter your transfer will be. A coat of varnish is recommended to protect colored pencil transfers.

You're almost guaranteed good transfer results if you brush a thin coat of liquid polymer clay onto the clay, and wait a few minutes for it to level out before placing your photo copy or colored pencil drawing directly onto the coated clay. Smooth the paper evenly to avoid air bubbles. (There's no need to burnish the back of the photocopy if you're using this method.) Let the piece sit for 10 to 15 minutes before baking 15 minutes at the clay manufacturer's recommended temperature. Remove the paper while the clay is still warm.

GALLERY

Top left: Sandra McCaw, *Winter Flower III,* Canework

Lower left: Luann Udell, *Lascaux Horse Necklaces,*
Polymer clay with antique trade beads and semi-precious stones

Top center: Krista Wells, *Three Masks,* Sculpted, handformed masks with canework

Above: Nan Roche, *Glyph Vessel,* Surface created with translucent overlay of polymer clay

Lower right: Nan Roche, *Chain Mail Collar,* Handformed polymer clay links

Upper right: Elise Winters, *Translucent/Reflective Screen,* Canework, mokume gane, etched acrylic paint

Upper left: Elise Winters, *Fan Brooch,* **Photo transfer, acrylic paint, and carving.** PHOTO BY PETER FORNABI

Upper right: Irene Semanchuk Dean, *Abstract Wall Piece,* **Faux ade, faux wood, mokume gane, texturing, and caneworking.**

Lower left: Irene Semanchuk Dean, *Fossil Box,* **Handformed with relief texture.** PHOTO BY TIM BARNWELL

Lower right: Elise Winter, *Shell Earrings,* **Skinner blend and etched acrylic paint.** PHOTO BY RALPH GABRINER

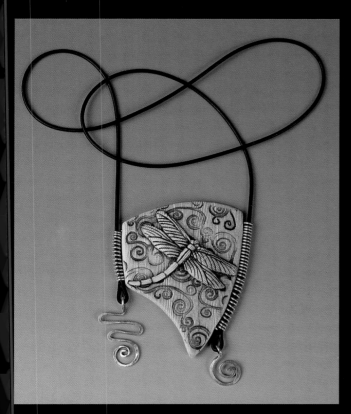

Upper left: Nan Roche, *Four Masks,* **Handformed polymer clay**

Lower left: Debbie Kreuger, *Dragonfly Pendant,* **Faux ivory**

Upper right: Irene Semanchuk Dean, *Tiled Clock,* **Skinner blend, faux wood, faux jade, mokume gane, stamping, and texturing.** Photo by Tim Barnwell

Lower right: Harriet Smith, Necklace with canework

Festive Salt and Pepper Shakers

Transform a pair of ordinary shakers with a covering of clay that melts from one color to the next.

Designer: Irene Semanchuk Dean

YOU WILL NEED

1 ounce (28 g) each of yellow, orange, and light green polymer clay

One teaspoon (5 g) black embossing powder (see page 17)

Pasta machine

Cutting blade

Set of glass salt and pepper shakers

Sheet of 80- or 100-grit coarse sandpaper

Small, square metal cutters (available at craft stores)

1 Blend the yellow, orange, and light green polymer clay to create a Skinner blend (see page 24). Lightly sprinkle the black embossing powder across the length of the clay several times while blending it, until the surface has a peppered look. Roll out the sheet out on the pasta machine to about ¹⁄₁₆ inch (1.5 mm). The sheet should be large enough to cover both of the shakers, or twice the circumference of one of the shakers in length and at least as wide as the height of the shakers.

2 Lay the sheet on your work surface so that the stripes are vertical. Cut through the center with the cutting blade from side to side. Position a shaker on one of the cut edges of the clay, adjusting the clay to the taper of the shaker. Roll the clay around it, pressing gently to ensure good adhesion and no air bubbles. When the roll is complete, press the overlapping end of the clay on top of the cut edge. Pull it back to reveal an indented line from the edge, and cut along this line before butting the two ends together. Press and smooth

the seam gently with your fingers. Use the cutting blade to trim excess clay from the top and bottom of each shaker, allowing room for the shaker top to be screwed on.

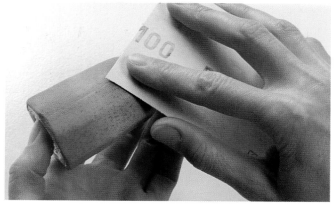

3 To texture the clay, hold the shakers between your fingers at the top and bottom (avoid touching the clay). Gently press a sheet of the coarse sandpaper repeatedly over the clay to create a rough surface, and meld the seam where the two ends meet. After texturing the clay, check the top and bottom edges, and trim away any distortions.

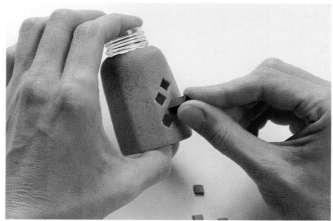

4 Use the small, square-shaped canapé cutters to create a series of peepholes around the center of each of the shakers. Remove the clay gently after cutting each hole, being careful not to disturb the surface. Bake for 30 minutes according to the clay manufacturer's instructions.

Mokume Gane Barrette and Earrings

Accidental occurences in the mokume gane process lend abstract beauty to these luxurious adornments.
Each surface is unique, and can't be replicated.

Designer: Irene Semanchuk Dean

1 Use the rolling pin or pasta machine to roll out conditioned sheets of the black and copper clays to about a ¹⁄₁₆-inch (1.5 mm) thickness. Roll out ¼ ounce (7 g) of the gold clay to the same thickness, and save the leftover gold clay. Use the cutting blade to trim each of the sheets to measure approximately 2 x 3 inches (5 x 7.5 cm). Cut four out of black, two out of copper, and two out of gold. Stack them like pancakes, alternating sheets of copper and gold between sheets of black to create a stack of about eight layers about ¼ inch (6 mm) thick. As you add each layer, roll it gently with the brayer in alternating directions to adhere it to the one below. During this process, flip the stack occasionally, and roll it on the other side to distribute the clay evenly.

2 Use a variety of similarly sized tools to make impressions in the stack of clay. (If you use canapé cutters, don't cut all the way through to the bottom of the stack; you want to make an impression of the shape without removing any clay.) Overlap and vary the depth of the impressions.

3 Press the stack firmly onto your work surface with your hands so that it does not move. Hold the slicing blade on either end, carefully draw it across the

top of the stack, and remove a thin layer of clay. Clean your blade between slices by wiping it across a paper towel slightly moistened with rubbing alcohol. Set the layer aside, and repeat this process to make several more slices. As you remove thin slices, patterns will emerge as the layers of clay are revealed.

4 Roll out a sheet from the leftover gold clay to about a ⅛-inch (3 mm) thickness. Arrange a mokume gane slice on top of this sheet of clay, covering an area at least as large as the barrette template. (You can overlap more than one slice, if needed.) Use a brayer or rolling pin to smooth the slices into the gold clay. Lay the barrette template on top of the clay, and cut out a shape. Lay the clay barrette shape on top of the metal barrette backing, and bake it for 30 minutes according to the clay manufacturer's instructions. After it cools, remove the clay, and wipe off the back of the clay and the metal barette backing with rubbing alcohol. Allow them to dry.

5 To make the earrings, roll a ¾-inch-diameter (1.9 cm) piece of gold clay into a sphere, pierce it with the skewer, and move it to the center. Gently roll the skewer and clay back and forth with your hands on your work surface until the clay is elongated into a 2-inch-wide (5 cm) tube. Cover the clay tube with small mokume gane slices. Continue rolling gently on your work surface until the slices are smoothed into the background. Position your cutting blade crosswise on top of the tube, then roll the tube slowly and evenly to create individual beads. Leave the beads on the skewer, and bake them for 20 minutes according to the clay manufacturer's directions. When the baked clay has cooled, wet sand the barrette and the beads on the skewer. Buff if desired. Glue the metal back onto the barrette. Place accent beads and polymer beads onto the headpins as shown in the finished photo, curl the headpins into loops with round-nose pliers, and attach the earring hooks.

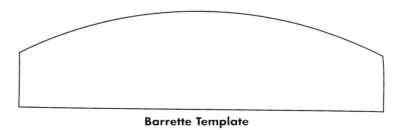

Barrette Template

Pressed Leaf Bookmarks

Collect your favorite leaves and save their intricate patterns on a bookmark

gilded with metallic mica powders.

Designer: Diane Villano

2 Remove the leaves from the wax paper. Use the small paintbrush to apply a light coat of the mica powder to one of the leaves. Gently tap off any excess powder.

1 Sandwich the leaves between sheets of wax paper, and place them between two books to flatten. Use the rolling pin or pasta machine to roll out the conditioned clay to about a ¹⁄₁₆-inch-thick (1.5 mm) sheet. Use the template and a cutting blade to cut out the bookmark. Use the drinking straw or small hole cutter to punch a hole about ⅓ inch (8 mm) from one of the short edges in the center.

3 Place the powdered side of the leaf on the clay bookmark. Gently rub it in place with your finger, then place a small piece of wax paper over the leaf. Lightly roll the brayer over the wax paper to transfer the powder and to emboss the clay with the leaf's texture. Remove the wax paper and leaf from the clay. Repeat steps 2 and 3 to add the imprints of more leaves until you are satisfied with your design. Bake the clay for 20 minutes according to the clay manufacturer's instructions. Remove them from the oven while they're still warm, and place them between books to flatten them.

4 After the bookmark has cooled, brush a light coat of varnish over the powdered areas. When the varnish is dry, gently rub your finger over the surface of the bookmark to check for complete coverage. If any powder comes off, apply a second coat of varnish.

VARIATIONS:

- Use more than one color of powder on the leaf— brush one color on the edges, another along the main vein, then blend. (Varnishing will make the colors bleed together slightly, which creates a nice effect. If you prefer that the colors don't bleed, varnish each color separately, allowing it to dry before varnishing the next one.)

- Cover the background of the bookmark with a different color of powder while the leaf is still in place. Varnish the leaves first, allow to dry, then varnish the background.

- Use two or more colors of clay marbled together as the base for the bookmark.

- Use patterned scissors to trim the edges of the baked bookmark.

- Choose leaves for your bookmark that coordinate with a book—such as herbs with a cookbook—to make an imaginative gift.

5 Fold the ribbon or cord in half, and thread the fold through the hole in the front of the bookmark, forming a 2-inch (5 cm) loop. Thread the ends through the loop and tighten the knot.

Blue Mica Jewelry

Luscious surfaces appear and disappear in the layers of this simple-to-make, but intriguing jewelry set.

Designer: Harriet Smith

1 Mix the scrap clay together with your hands or with the pasta machine until it is all of a uniform color. Roll it out with the rolling pin or pasta machine to a ¹⁄₁₆ inch (1.5 mm) thickness. Emboss the surface of the clay with a row of three impressions of the square stamp and three impressions of the circular stamp.

2 Use your fingertip to pick up a very small amount of blue powdered mica pigment. Tap your finger gently to remove the excess powder. Gently apply the powder to the three square impressions and the surrounding surface with your finger. (Don't use a brush because it allows the powder to fall into the indented portion of the clay impression.) Apply powder to the center portion only of the three circular impressions (you'll be layering clay on top of these pieces later).

4 Lift, move, and place the square pieces onto the circular pieces.

3 Trim around each of the embossed pieces with your cutting blade or craft knife to form square shapes. (Your pieces will be trimmed later, so it's not necessary to make perfectly neat edges.) Use the canapé cutter or other cutter in a shape of your choice to remove the centers from the square-shaped pieces.

5 To make a pin, place these two layers on top of a third layer of scrap clay in the diagonal configuration shown. Place a piece of paper or wax paper on top before gently pressing the layers together. Trim around the shapes to create a pin. Follow steps 1 through 5 to create two squares for earrings. Bake the pin and earring squares for 20 minutes according to the clay manufacturer's instructions. When cool, move the jewelry outside, and lightly spray the tops of the squares with two to three coats of matte varnish. Wipe off the backs of the pin back and earring posts with rubbing alcohol, allow to dry, and glue them into place on the pin and earrings.

Mokume Gane Ceiling Fan Pull

Adopt an ancient Japanese metalworking technique to polymer clay, and create wondrous surfaces that look like precious stones.

Designer: Irene Semanchuk Dean

YOU WILL NEED

Small amounts of lime green, turquoise, and purple polymer clay

1 ounce (28 g) of translucent polymer clay

½ ounce (14 g) of solid color polymer clay

Rolling pin or pasta machine

Wax paper

Package of silver-colored metal leaf (see page 16)

Golf tee, screw, canapé cutter, pen, or other objects to make indentations in clay

Cutting blade

Paper towel

Rubbing alcohol

Skewer or knitting needle

Brass ball chain and connector (as used for fan pulls, available at hardware stores)

Liquid polymer clay or cyanoacrylate glue

600- and 800-grit wet/dry sandpaper

Soft buffing cloth

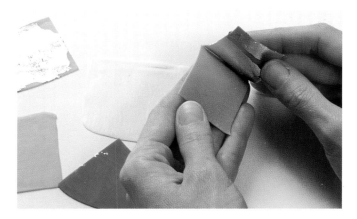

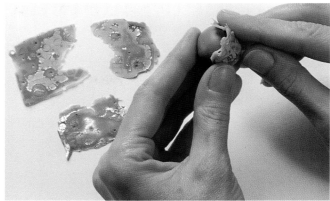

1 Mix each of the small amounts of colored clays with ¼ ounce (7 g) of translucent clay to make tinted translucent clays. Use a rolling pin or pasta machine to roll out six to eight paper-thin sheets of the clays between two pieces of wax paper. Remove a sheet of the silver-colored metal leaf from the packaging, lay a sheet of clay down on it, and pull away the excess leaf. Continue this process to add leaf to one side of about half of the tinted translucent sheets of clay. Sandwich metal-leafed sheets between tinted translucent sheets to make a stack, pressing each layer gently as you add it. Top the stack off with a translucent sheet, so that all the metal leaf is enclosed in the polymer clay.

3 Roll the solid color clay into a small ball of the size that you want your fan pull. Apply and overlap the mokume gane slices until you have a pleasing arrangement. As you apply the slices, gently roll the ball between your palms without distorting the clay until it is spherical.

2 Use objects such as a golf tee, the rounded end of a pen, or canapé cutters to make deep, closely placed indentations in the clay. Press the stack of clay firmly onto your work surface to prevent it from moving. Hold the cutting blade at each end, and draw it across the top of the stack to remove thin, irregular slices that reveal random patterns of color and metal leaf. Clean the blade on a paper towel with a little rubbing alcohol on it between each cut. Set the slices aside.

4 Use the skewer or knitting needle to make a hole about ½ inch (1.3 cm) deep into the clay. Apply a small amount of liquid polymer clay or cyanoacrylate glue to the last two balls on the length of ball chain. Push this end of the ball chain into the hole, and feed it downwards so that about ½ inch (1.3 cm) of chain is in the hole. Push the chain deeper into the hole with the skewer, if needed. Gently use your fingers or a sculpting tool to move clay and close the hole around the chain. Bake for 30 minutes according to the clay manufacturer's instructions. When cool, sand with wet/dry sandpaper, and buff with a soft cloth. (Avoid using a buffing wheel, which might catch the chain and be dangerous.)

Fake Slate Frame

No one will belive that this frame isn't really made of stone,
until they notice how light it is!

Designer: Diane Villano

YOU WILL NEED

2 ounces (56 g) of black polymer clay

Small, unpainted wooden frame in size of your choice

Heat-resistant PVA glue

Small paintbrush (optional)

Rolling pin or pasta machine

Cutting blade

Gray acrylic paint

Paper towels

1 Use your fingers or the small paintbrush to apply a light coat of heat-resistant PVA glue to the frame. Allow it to dry. Use the rolling pin or pasta machine to roll the black clay out to a 1/16 inch (1.5 mm) thickness (#4 thickness on the Atlas pasta machine). Tear small pieces of the clay from the sheet, and apply them to the frame, overlapping the edges as needed. Aim for a ragged, organic appearance.

3 Use your fingertips or a small brush to apply gray acrylic paint on a small section of the frame.

2 Cover the frame completely on the front and sides. Smooth away any fingerprints, then use a cutting blade placed flush with the back of the frame to trim off the excess clay. After trimming, bake the frame for 20 minutes according to the clay manufacturer's instructions, and allow it to cool.

4 Quickly wipe the excess paint off with paper towels, so that paint remains only in the creases. Continue until the entire frame is completed. Allow it to dry completely.

Variations:

Try terra-cotta colored clay with a light gray paint wash, or dark green clay with copper paint.

Molded Buttons

Transform a humdrum shirt or dress with colorful buttons made to suit any mood.
The possibilities are endless!

Designer: Irene Semanchuk Dean

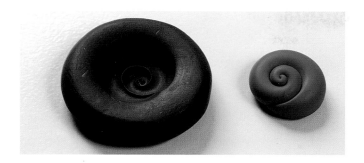

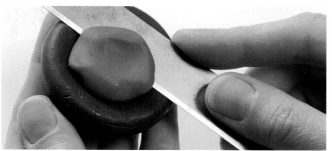

1 Condition 1 ounce (28 g) of durable clay, and roll it into a ball. (If you're using scraps of different colors, condition them until they are one color.) Place the clay on a piece of wax paper, and use a jar lid or other flat object to flatten it evenly until it is about ¾ inch (1.9 cm) thick. Use a small brush to apply cornstarch to the object. Press the object firmly, without twisting it, into the clay. Remove the object from the clay. Bake the mold for an hour at the clay manufacturer's recommended temperature.

3 Use a slicing blade to slice any excess clay off of the top. After pressing the clay into the mold and trimming it, leave it in the mold. Use the needle-nose pliers to unfold a vinyl-covered paper clip, and follow with wire cutters to cut off a short piece of wire that measures about ¾ inch (1.9 cm).

Tip:

After you've molded and trimmed your first button, remove the clay and roll it into a ball. Use this piece of clay as a guide to determine how much clay to use for subsequent buttons.

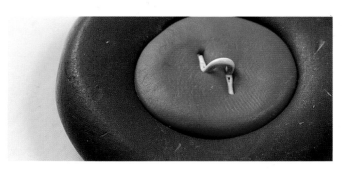

2 To form a short cone shape from the clay that is proportional to your mold, begin with a ball of clay, and roll it into a blunt point. Brush the mold with cornstarch or water. Place the point of the cone in the center of the mold, and press the clay into it.

Tips for cleaning garments with clay buttons:

- Clay buttons need special care when washing. You may find that you prefer to hand-wash a garment that has clay buttons, although turning it inside out when machine washing it should provide sufficient protection.

- If using a washing machine, run a test button through a wash load to see how it will hold up, especially if it's covered with varnish or sealer.

- Air dry garments with clay buttons. Do not dry clean clay buttons.

4 Use needle-nose pliers to curl the wire into a U shape, then bend out the legs at the halfway point. (These "feet" prevent the wire from pulling out of the clay.) Invert the wire piece, and press the feet into the clay until the feet are covered. Leave a wire loop large enough to insert a needle and thread later. Use a sculpting tool, golf tee, or any other bluntly pointed object to smooth the clay around the wire. Remove the button from the mold, and cradle it right side up on polyester fiberfill or a wadded paper towel. Bake for 30 minutes according to the clay manufacturer's directions. Sand and buff your buttons if you want a shine.

Faux Wood Letter Opener

Any recipient of this letter opener will appreciate its refinement and good taste.

Designer: Irene Semanchuk Dean

YOU WILL NEED
1 ounce (28 g) champagne polymer clay, or 1 ounce (28 g) translucent polymer clay mixed with a pinch of tan or ecru clay
Small amounts of red and purple polymer clay
Pasta machine or rolling pin
Short stack of books
Metal letter opener (available at office supply stores)
Craft knife
Scissors
Wax paper
Various objects to make impressions in the clay such as a coiled piece of wire, rubber stamps, or sculpting tools
Brown or burnt umber acrylic paint
Paper towel

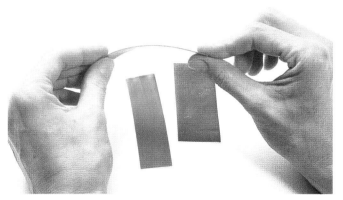

1 With a rolling pin or very narrow setting on the pasta machine, roll the red and purple polymer clay out into two paper-thin sheets that each measure 1 inch (2.5 cm) square. Bake the squares for 10 minutes at the clay manufacturer's recommended temperature, and remove them from the oven while they're still warm. Place books on top to flatten them out while they cool.

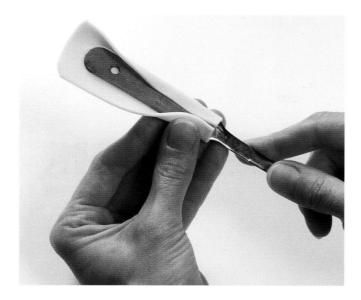

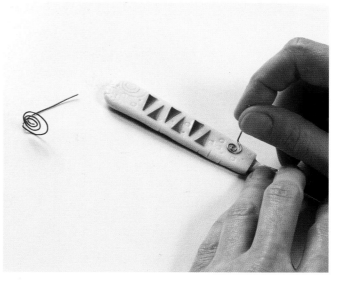

2 Roll the champagne-colored clay into a sheet slightly less than ⅛-inch (3 mm) thickness. Lay the handle of the metal letter opener onto this sheet, and use the craft knife to trim a piece of clay that will fit around it. Form the clay around the handle of the letter opener, smooth the seam, and trim away any excess clay.

4 Use objects of your choice (such as rubber stamps or sculpting tools) to create impressions and indentations in the clay. Add marks along the edges and back side of the handle to simulate weathered wood.

3 Use scissors to cut the baked, cooled sheets of purple and red clay into small triangular shapes to be used for inlay. Arrange them in alternating colors and positions on the clay covering of the letter opener handle, and gently press them in until they are flush with the surface. (To prevent fingerprints on the clay, cover the surface with a piece of wax paper before pressing.)

5 Bake the letter opener for 20 minutes at the clay manufacturer's recommended temperature. When cool, rub brown acrylic paint with your fingers over the handle and into all the indentations. Immediately wipe off any excess paint with a paper towel.

Faux Bronze Light Switch Plate

This elegant light switch plate elevates the use of the rubber stamp to an art!

Designer: Debbie Kreuger

1 Use the rolling pin or pasta machine to roll out the conditioned dark green clay to a ⅛-inch-thick (3 mm) sheet that measures about 4 inches (10 cm) square. Carefully press the clay onto the sheet of gold leaf before flipping it over.

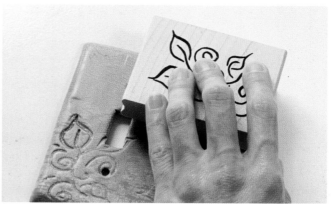

2 Roll out a paper-thin sheet of the conditioned translucent clay (#6 or thinner setting on an Atlas machine). Lay the sheet on top of the gold-leafed sheet of green clay. To crackle the gold leaf, run the layered clay through the pasta machine at the thickest setting, or roll it in one direction with the rolling pin to about a ⅛-inch (3 mm) thickness. Turn the clay a quarter turn. Run it back through the pasta machine to form a ⅟₁₆-inch-thick (1.5 mm) sheet, or roll it to this thickness with a rolling pin turned to a position perpendicular to the original rolling direction.

4 Dampen the rubber stamp with a wet sponge, and press the stamp into the clay. Repeat this process to emboss the surface with a pleasing pattern. Bake the plate for 30 minutes according to the clay manufacturer's instructions. After it cools, wet-sand the surface of the switch plate with 400-grit wet/dry sandpaper.

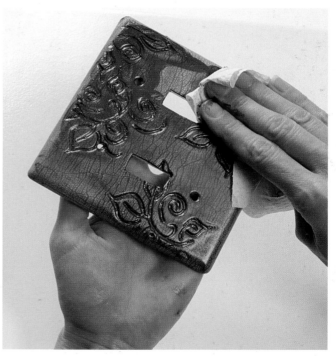

3 Lay the clay on top of the light switch plate, smoothing out any air bubbles by pressing gently from the center out towards the edges. Trim away the excess clay from the edges and the switch holes with a craft knife. Use a pencil or golf tee to poke the clay out of the screw holes.

5 Dry it off thoroughly with a paper towel, and apply bronze acrylic paint to the surface with your fingers, making sure to get paint into every groove created by the rubber stamp. Wipe away the excess paint with a paper towel, and allow it to dry completely. Wet-sand the surface with 800-grit paper, then dry it off. To set the paint, bake the plate for 10 minutes at 250° F (121° C). Buff the surface with a soft cloth.

Faux Jade Bowl

This shallow, decorative bowl that simulates jade is incised with a pattern reminiscent of Mayan designs.

Designer: Irene Semanchuk Dean

Design template (page 52)

3 ounces (84 g) of translucent polymer clay

¼ ounce (7 g) of green polymer clay mixed with a small portion of black polymer clay to make olive green clay

Small portion of black polymer clay for grating

Black embossing powder

Small section of window screen or a food grater (use with clay only)

Rolling pin or pasta machine

Craft knife

Coarse sandpaper

4-inch-wide (10 cm), ovenproof ceramic or glass bowl

400-, 600-, 800-, and 1000-grit sheets of wet/dry sandpaper

Ballpoint pen

V-shaped printmaking gouge made for cutting linoleum block (found at art supply stores)

Raw sienna acrylic paint

Paper towel

Buffing wheel or soft cloth

Cyanoacrylate glue or liquid polymer clay

Sculpting or shaping tool

2 Flatten the wad of clay into a roughly circular shape with the palm of your hand and fingers. Grate the black clay on the window screen or the grater to create small flecks on the green clay. Press them in gently with the palm of your hand. Turn the clay over, and add black flecks to the other side. Flatten the clay further by rolling it out with the rolling pin, or running it through the pasta machine to ⅛-inch (3 mm) thickness. Lay it on your work surface, and cut out a circular shape with the craft knife. Remove the excess clay, and set it aside. Use your fingers to gently smooth the cut edges. Add a bit of texture by pressing the coarse sandpaper randomly on both sides of the clay.

1 Divide the translucent clay into four pieces on your work surface. Mix varying amounts of the olive green clay into each of the pieces of translucent clay to make a range of light and dark shades. Mix a small amount of black embossing powder into two of the lighter shades of clay. Combine the clay into one clump, and mix together lightly, leaving the clay mottled rather than thoroughly mixed.

3 Turn the ovenproof bowl upside down on your work surface, and place the circular clay on top of it to create a gentle slope to the clay edges. Bake both together for 30 minutes according to the clay manufacturer's instructions. After the clay has cooled, remove it from the ovenproof bowl. Sand both sides of the clay bowl with 400-grit wet/dry sandpaper, and dry it off thoroughly.

4 Use the template below as a guide, or make up your own design, and sketch it directly onto your baked clay with a ballpoint pen. (These lines will be sanded off after carving the surface of the clay.)

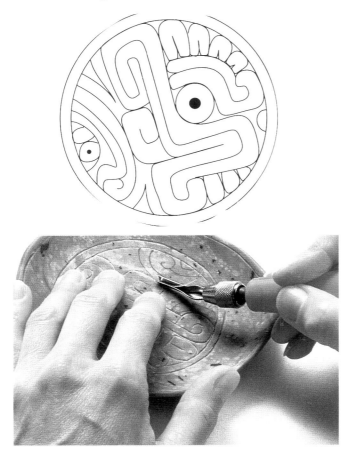

5 Use the V-shaped gouge to follow and incise the lines for your design. Brush away the clay shavings as they accumulate. (At any point during your carving, you can use 400-grit wet/dry sandpaper to sand away pen markings, and redraw the rest of your design.)

Tips:

- If you've never carved with a linoleum gouge before, practice first on a sheet of baked clay. Try making straight lines, curves, spirals, and other shapes.

- To make curved lines, hold the gouge firmly in place, and move the clay in the direction of the curve, rather than pushing the gouge.

- When carving, be careful where your fingers are in relation to the cutter so that you don't get cut.

- Work slowly and carefully to keep the gouge from slipping and cutting an unintentional line.

6 When you are satisfied with your image, brush away all bits of excess clay. Sand the bowl with 400-, 600-, 800-grit wet/dry sandpaper, respectively. Dry the bowl thoroughly. Use your fingers to rub burnt sienna acrylic paint into the carved lines. Wipe away excess paint immediately with a paper towel. Allow the paint to dry completely. After the paint has dried, sand the bowl again with 800-grit wet/dry sandpaper to remove any excess paint. For a high shine, buff the bottom of the bowl on a cotton buffing wheel, or use a soft cloth and lots of elbow grease.

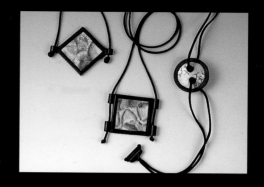

7 Use the clay you set aside in step 2 to make legs for the bowl. Divide the clay into four equal pieces, and roll each into a cone shape. Manipulate the clay to form curled feet on the legs. Flatten the thick end of each cone by pushing it onto your work surface. Reposition the bowl upside down on the bottom of the ceramic bowl. Brush the flat end of each leg with cyanoacrylate glue or liquid polymer clay, and press it into place on the bottom of the bowl.

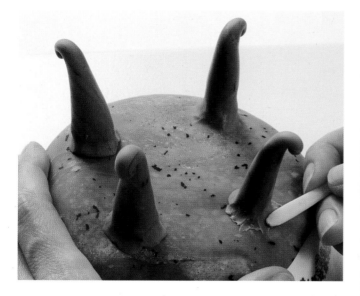

8 Use a sculpting or shaping tool to feather the clay around the top of each leg. Bake the bowl for 30 minutes according to the clay manufacturer's directions. When cool, gently wet sand the legs with 400, 600-, 800-, and then 1000-grit sandpaper. Buff the top of the bowl on a buffing wheel or by hand with a soft cloth. (Don't attempt to buff the legs on a wheel.)

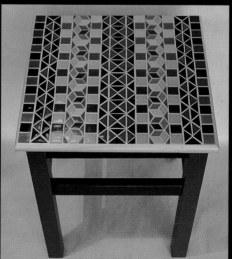

Top: Julia Sober, *Chromatic Pendants,* Colored pencil transfer.

Middle: Bob Paris and Nancy Bundy, Pin and earrings with canework

Bottom: Krista Wells, *Royal Court Jester Table,* Skinner blend, handpiecing

Cabinet Knobs

A kaleidoscope of colors adorns the surface of these eye-popping cabinet knobs !

Designer: Harriet Smith

YOU WILL NEED

Polymer clay cane (a small, triangular-shaped cane is used here)

Scrap polymer clay in color to match cane slices

Wooden cabinet knobs

100-, 400-, and 600-grit sandpaper

Heat-resistant PVA glue

Rolling pin or pasta machine

Cutting blade

400- and 600-grit sandpaper

Soft cloth for buffing

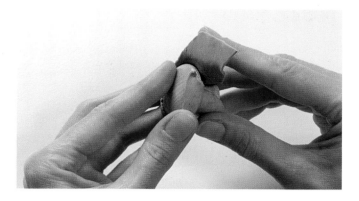

1 Sand away any rough spots from the wooden knobs with the 100-grit sandpaper. Use your fingertips to cover the knobs with a light coat of heat-resistant PVA glue. Apply the glue to the tops first, and allow them to dry before covering the sides. After the knobs are completely dry, use the pasta machine or the rolling pin to roll out conditioned scrap clay to a ¹⁄₁₆-inch (1.5 mm) thickness. Lay the clay sheet on your work surface, and cut out a rectangle slightly longer than the circumference of one of the knobs and wider than its side. Gently stretch the clay around the neck of the knob, being careful to press out any air bubbles. Trim the clay with the cutting blade so that the two ends meet in a butt joint. Smooth the seam with your fingertips until it disappears.

3 Slice the cane into at least six slices, and position them on top of the knob in a configuration of your choice, then gently press the slices onto the top of the knob. Place the knob top down on your work surface, and gently roll it in circles to smooth out the clay. Lightly burnish the clay with your fingertips to get rid of any fingerprint smudges. Bake the knob 30 minutes according to clay manufacturer's instructions. After it cools, wet-sand it with 400-grit followed by 600-grit sandpaper. (To prevent the wood from swelling, don't immerse the knob in water or get the back too wet.) Buff the clay lightly with a soft cloth.

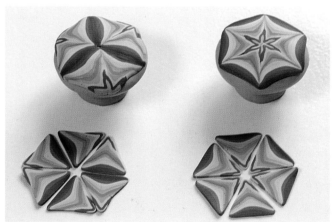

2 Position the cutting blade flush with the back of the knob, and trim off any excess clay. Trim the clay on the top of the knob. (When you apply the cane slices to the top of the cabinet knob, you'll have a smooth, rounded top.)

4 Create the same design on subsequent knobs, or try out different configurations of the slices.

EMBOSSED NOTEPAD

This lovely notepad cover creates the illusion of a sky filled with snowflakes and stars.

Designer: Heather Roselli

YOU WILL NEED
Blue pearl and pearl white polymer clay, 1½ ounce (42 g) each (choose a strong, flexible brand)
3- x 5-inch (7.5 x 12.5 cm) spiral notepad
Pliers
Rubber band
Pasta machine
White paper
Cutting blade
Small round cutter or plastic coffee stirring stick
Snowflake and star stamps
Talcum powder
Stack of books
400-, 600-, 800-grit sandpaper (optional)
Buffing cloth (optional)

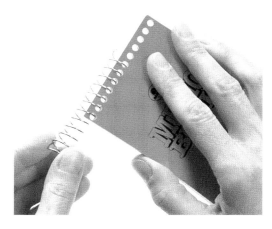

1 Use the pliers to gently straighten out the bent wire end on one side of the spiral notepad, and twist the wire out of its holes. Secure the pages and the back cover with a rubber band to keep the holes aligned.

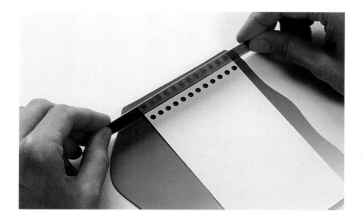

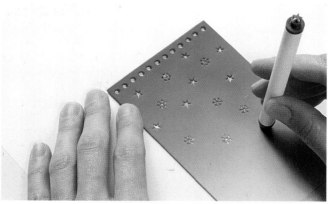

2 Create a Skinner blend from the blue pearl and pearl white polymer clay (see page 24). Use the rolling pin or pasta machine to roll out the clay to a ¹⁄₁₆-inch (1.5 mm) thickness. Place the sheet of clay right side up on clean white paper. Smooth out any air bubbles between the clay and paper. Lay the notepad's cardboard cover right side up on the clay sheet. Use the cutting blade to trim the clay about ¹⁄₁₆ inch (1.5 mm) larger than the cover on all sides except the top. Trim along the edge of the cover's top. To achieve a clean cut edge in the clay, press the blade straight down, rather than dragging it.

4 Dip the snowflake stamp into talcum powder, and stamp the image randomly onto the clay with firm, even pressure. Repeat this process with the star stamp to create a pattern. Be careful not to push the stamp through the clay.

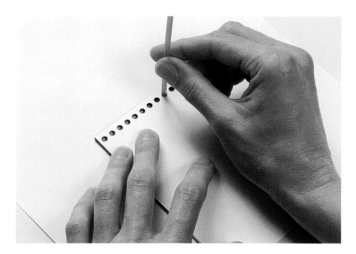

3 With the cardboard cover still in place, use a small round cutter or a plastic coffee stirring stick to remove the clay from the holes along the top. (Trim off the end of the plastic stirring stick as it fills with clay to maintain a clean cut.) Remove the cardboard cover from the clay.

5 When you've completed the stamping, bake the clay on the paper for 30 minutes at the manufacturer's recommended temperature. (Removing the clay from the paper before baking may distort it, resulting in an odd fit.) Remove the clay from the oven while it is still warm, and place a stack of books on top of it to keep it flat while it cools. After it cools, sand and buff the cover if desired. Realign the clay cover with the paper pages and backing, and carefully screw the spiral of wire into the pad. Bend the end of the wire to hold it in place.

Steamin' Hot Coffee Pin

Translucent clay laced with glitter creates a magical surface on this photo transfer pin.

Designer: Debbie Krueger

Photocopy of coffee cup pattern (below)

½ ounce (14 g) of white polymer clay

1 ounce (28 g) of fuchsia or magenta polymer clay for backing

Small amounts of purple and lavendar polymer clay

6 thin slices of checkerboard cane (see page 23)

Rolling pin or pasta machine

Scissors

Cutting blade

600- and 800-grit wet/dry sandpaper

Metal spoon

Colored pencils in the following colors: black, brown, violet, purple

½ ounce (14 g) translucent polymer clay

Glitter (iridescent or semi-transparent color)

Wax paper

Soft cloth or buffing wheel

Rubbing alcohol

Pin back

Cyanoacrylate glue

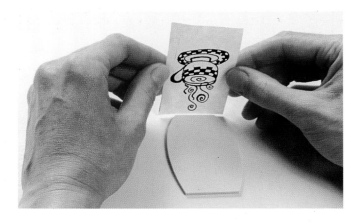

1 Use the rolling pin or pasta machine to roll out the conditioned white clay to a ⅛ inch (3 mm) thickness. Lay the clay on your work surface. Cut out the coffee cup pattern/pin template with scissors. Place the template on the clay, and trim around it with the cutting blade. Remove the excess clay and set the photocopied template aside. Gently press the 800-grit sandpaper onto the surface of the clay to create a good drawing surface after it's baked. Lay the photocopied coffee cup pattern face down on the clay, burnish the back with the spoon, and allow it to sit for 10 minutes. Bake the clay for 10 minutes at the manufacturer's suggested temperature. Remove the pattern after baking, before it has cooled.

2 When the clay has cooled, color the design with colored pencils. Darken the color by adding several layers of color. Use the black pencil to reinforce the lines from the photocopy transfer.

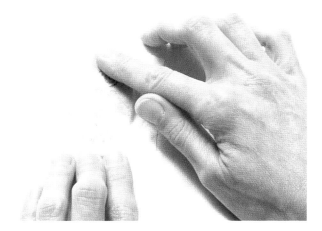

onto it. Roll out a thin length or snake of purple clay long enough to frame the pin. Gently push it into place around the edge of the pin on top of the bottom layer of clay.

3 Condition ½ ounce (14 g) of translucent clay, incorporating ¼ teaspoon (1.5 g) of glitter until it is evenly distributed. Roll the clay into a paper-thin sheet on your pasta machine (make it cardstock thin if rolling the clay by hand). If you find that the clay is too sticky, you may have better results rolling the clay between two sheets of wax paper. Lay this thin, glittered sheet on top of the colored surface of your pin. Place a piece of wax paper on top. Press firmly from the center out towards the edges to remove air bubbles. Peel off the wax paper. Trim away the excess glittered clay. Bake the pin for 15 minutes according to the clay manufacturer's instructions. Allow it to cool, then wet-sand with 600-grit followed by 800-grit sandpaper until the surface is smooth (see page 19). Buff it with a soft cloth or on a buffing wheel.

5 Roll out a thin snake of lavender clay, and press it into place on top of the first band. Trim the bottom layer of clay around the edge of the pin, leaving the bands intact.

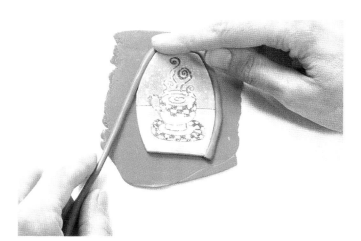

4 Use the rolling pin or pasta machine to roll out a piece of fuschia or magenta clay that is ⅟₁₆ inch (1.5 mm) thick and slightly wider than the pin. Lay the clay on a piece of wax paper, and press the pin firmly

6 Press the thin slices of checkerboard cane into place around the edges of the pin. Bake for 20 minutes according to the clay manufacturer's instructions. After the pin cools, wipe the back of the pin and the pin back with rubbing alcohol to remove oils. Attach the pin back with cyanoacrylate glue.

Glittering Pen

Save this beautiful, shimmering pen for your most personal correspondence.
You'll be inspired every time you use it!

Designer: Irene Semanchuk Dean

Pen with a gray or white plastic barrel
(clear barrels will warp)

Pliers (optional)

1 ounce (28 g) fuchsia polymer clay

1 ounce (28 g) blue polymer clay

Pasta machine

Cutting blade

Straightedge or ruler

Glitter in assorted colors (test before using, see page 17)

Wax paper

Index card

Scissors

Craft knife

Cellophane tape

Paper towel or polyester fiberfill

Small paintbrush

Varnish (see page 19)

100-grit sandpaper (optional)

Translucent liquid polymer clay (optional)

2 Roll the clay around the pen, then trim the clay with the cutting blade, and butt the edges together. Pinch the clay at the top end closed. Smooth out the seam that is formed, and roll the pen gently on your work surface to ensure good adhesion. Trim off any excess clay at the bottom of the pen. If any air bubbles are evident, slice them open, and reseal the clay.

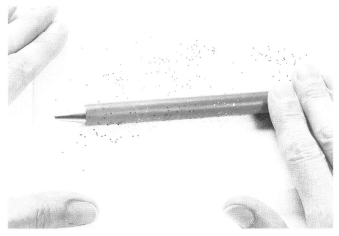

3 Spread approximately ½ teaspoon (2.5 g) of glitter onto a sheet of wax paper. Roll the clay-covered pen in the glitter until it is coated. Once the glitter has adhered, roll the pen on your work surface again to press in the glitter. Fold the index card into an M shape, and set the pen in the trough to bake. Bake for 30 minutes at the clay manufacturer's recommended temperature. Allow the pen to cool.

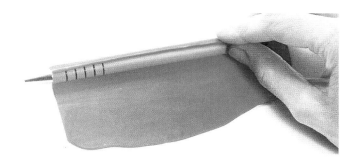

1 Remove the ink cartridge from the pen, and set it aside. (Depending on the brand, either screw it out or remove it with pliers.) Combine the blue and fuchsia clay to make a Skinner blend (see page 24). Use the rolling pin or pasta machine to roll about half of the clay to a ¹⁄₁₆-inch (1.5 mm) thickness. Use the cutting blade and a straightedge or ruler to cut one clean edge that is at least the length of the pen barrel. Lay the pen barrel along the cut edge, and trim the clay perpendicular to the length to fit the barrel at both ends. Trim the top to about ⅛" longer.

4 To make the cap, cut a narrow piece of wax paper that will wrap around the pen in a single layer. Tape it tightly closed. Use the remaining clay to roll out a sheet that is $\frac{1}{16}$ inch (1.5 mm) thick. Use the cutting blade to trim a 2-inch-wide (5 cm) strip from it that is long enough to roll around the circumference of the pen. Place the pen onto this sheet, roll the clay sheet around, and butt the edges as you did in the first step. Leave this clay cap on the pen, and coat it with glitter as described in step 2. Bake the pen with the cap on it for 15 minutes. After it cools completely, twist and pull gently to remove the cap from the pen.

5 To make an end for the cap, place one end of it onto a small sheet of $\frac{1}{8}$-inch-thick (3 mm) clay, and cut around it with the craft knife to make an end for the cap. Press the cap into place on the end of the pen. Press the end of the cap into the glitter to coat it. Gently stuff a small piece of paper towel or fiberfill into the cap, and bake it for 15 minutes at the clay manufacturer's recommended temperature. To prevent the glitter from flaking off, use the small paintbrush to apply two coats of varnish to the pen and the cap. Allow the varnish to dry thoroughly. Replace the cartridge before placing the cap on the pen.

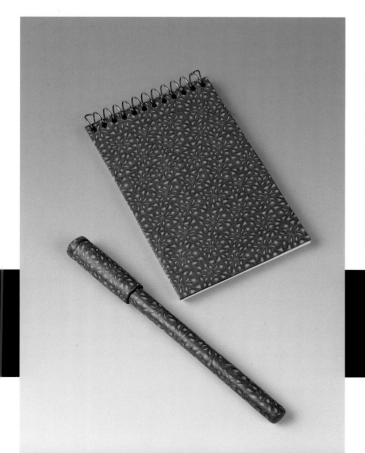

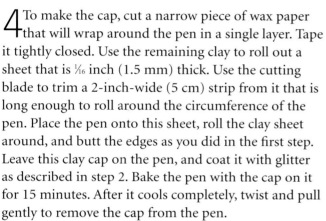

Tips:

- If the cap is too small in diameter and won't fit onto the pen, you can enlarge the interior by scraping a few times with a small piece of rolled sandpaper.

- If the cap is too large for the pen, brush the inside of the cap with a thin layer of translucent liquid polymer clay, or smear a little polymer clay on the interior. Rebake the cap for 15 minutes.

Heather Roselli, Notepad and pen with canework

Silver Heart Box

Start with a humble cookie cutter and end up with a sexy, richly decorated box for candy, jewelry, or romantic tokens.

Designer: Heather Roselli

2 Place the baked heart onto the remaining sheet of silver clay, and trim around the edges with the craft knife to create a bottom for the box. Remove the excess clay. Lightly press the walls of the heart into the clay bottom, and smooth the clay with your fingertips to seal the edges.

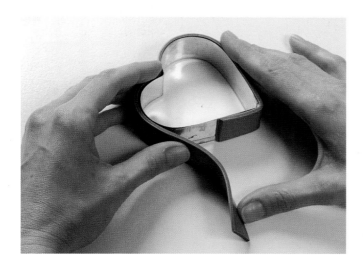

1 Use the rolling pin or the pasta machine to roll a portion of the silver polymer clay to about a ⅛-inch (3 mm) thickness. From this sheet, cut a strip that is 8 to 10 inches (20 to 25 cm) long and 1 inch (2.5 cm) wide. Brush the outside of the heart-shaped cutter with cornstarch. Wrap the strip around the outside of the cutter, and cut away the excess clay where the ends of the strip meet. Smooth the seam with your fingertips. Bake the heart for 15 minutes at the clay manufacturer's recommended temperature. After the cutter and clay cool, carefully remove the clay from the cutter.

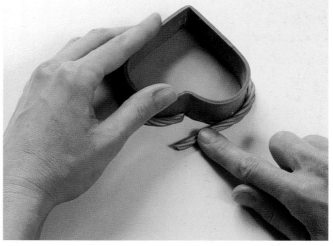

3 Use the clay gun fitted with a clover-shaped disc to extrude a rope of silver clay about ¼ inch (6 mm) wide and long enough to fit around the bottom of the heart. Evenly twist the clay rope, and apply half of it to one side of the bottom of the heart. Press gently to ensure good contact. Apply the other half of the rope to the other side of the heart. Where the rope ends butt together, trim them at an angle to form neat seams. Bake this assemblage for 30 minutes at the clay manufacturer's recommended temperature.

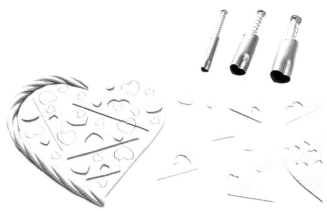

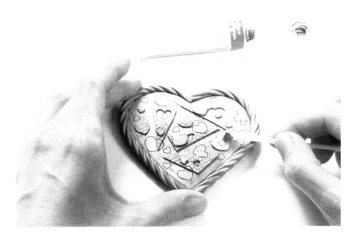

4 Roll out another sheet of the silver clay to a ⅛-inch (3 mm) thickness. Use the heart-shaped cutter to cut a shape that will become the box's lid. Roll the remaining clay to a ¹⁄₁₆-inch (1.5 mm) thickness. Add texture to this sheet of clay with the texturing materials. Use the craft knife to cut out an assortment of triangular shapes, and the small cutters to cut out an assortment of hearts from both the triangles and the remaining clay. Apply them randomly to the lid in a pleasing arrangement as shown. Use the small cutters to incise more heart patterns on the lid. Extrude another clover-shaped length of silver clay from the clay gun, twist it, and apply it to the edges of the lid as you did the box bottom.

6 After the box has cooled, thin the charcoal acrylic paint with water to make a wash. Apply the wash with a clean cotton swab one section at a time to areas of the box and lid, immediately wiping away excess paint with a paper towel from the higher areas. Allow the paint to dry completely, then use another cotton swab or your finger to apply the wax finish to the highest, textured areas. (A little goes a long way!) Allow to set for 30 minutes, then buff the entire piece lightly with a soft cloth or paper towel. Seal with the varnish.

5 Change the disc in the clay gun to a round one that is about ⅛ inch (3 mm) in diameter, and extrude a length of silver clay that is long enough to fit the edge of the heart's lid. Gently turn the lid over, and position the rope of clay just inside the edge of the lid to create a flange. Press gently but firmly enough to ensure good contact. Turn the lid face up, and bake it for 30 minutes according to the clay manufacturer's instructions.

Multi-Patterned Kite Magnet

Use readymade canes or create your own to make into this whimsical, colorful kite that flies safely out of harm's way on your refrigerator door.

Designer: Diane Villano

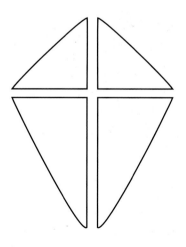

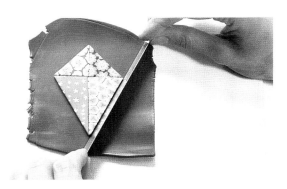

1 Use the rolling pin or pasta machine to roll out half of the purple clay out to a ⅟₁₆-inch (1.5 mm) thickness. Cut very thin slices from one of the canes, and place them onto the sheet of clay, covering an area the size of one triangular section of the kite template.

2 Place a piece of wax paper over the cane slices, and roll over the clay with the brayer or rolling pin until the seams between the slices disappear. Lay the triangle on top of the cane-covered section, and cut around it with the cutting blade. (To create a clean clay edge, hold the blade perpendicularly as you push it down, rather than dragging it.) Repeat this process by using the other three canes and triangular sections to create the remaining sections of the kite.

3 Position the four triangles together as shown in the photo, and gently press them into place to form a kite. Bake the sections for 20 minutes at the clay manufacturer's recommended temperature. Allow the clay to cool.

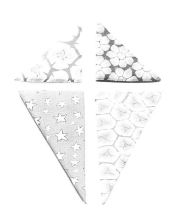

4 Roll the other half of the purple clay out to a ⅛-inch (3 mm) thickness. Lay it out on your work surface, and place the clay kite on top of it. Press the kite gently with your fingertips to adhere it to the clay. Use your cutting blade to trim around the edges of the kite, and remove the excess purple clay.

5 Use the nippers or wire cutters to cut an eye pin to a total length of ¾ inch (1.9 cm), and insert it into the clay backing at the bottom point of the kite. Bake the kite for 20 minutes according to the clay manufacturer's instructions, and allow it to cool. Remove the eye pin, apply a drop of cyanoacrylate glue to it, and reinsert it into the hole in the kite. Insert one end of the ribbon through the eye pin, and knot it close to the edge of the kite. Glue the magnet to the back of the kite. (For a variation, glue a pin back onto the kite instead of a magnet.)

Snowflake Ornaments

Appealing symmetry adorns these beveled-edged ornaments that are beautiful yet simple to make.

Designer: Jody Bishel

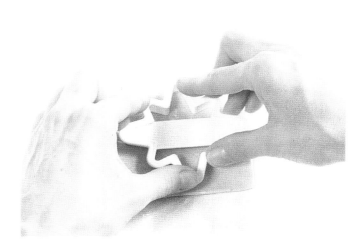

1 Condition the pearl white clay (see pages 9, 10), and roll out a ⅛-inch-thick (3 mm) thick sheet on the thickest setting of the pasta machine. Cover the clay with a sheet of plastic wrap, and smooth it out. Press the snowflake cookie cutter through the plastic wrap and clay to cut out several ornaments. Remove the plastic wrap and make a small hole with the needle tool or

skewer at the top of each for inserting the hanging cord later. Bake the ornament 20 minutes according to clay manufacturer's instructions.

2 In a small waxed paper cup, mix 1 tablespoon (15 ml) of transparent liquid polymer clay with a pea-sized amount of gold mica powder. In another cup, mix 1 tablespoon (15 ml) of transparent liquid polymer clay with a tiny amount of black oil paint. (If you would like a little sparkle in the black, add some silver mica powder to the mixture.) When the baked ornaments have cooled, brush a light coat of uncolored transparent liquid polymer clay onto one of the ornaments. Position the snowflake template next to it. Use a needle tool, skewer, or ball-ended sculpting tool to drop dots of the gold and black liquid polymer clay onto the surface, using the template as a guide.

Tip:

When you're making a dot, a thread of transparent liquid polymer clay will form between the surface and the needle tool or skewer. If you lift the needle tool or skewer straight up slowly, it will break and flow back into the dot. If you pull away too fast or at an angle, it will spoil the dot. Mistakes can be carefully wiped off with a paper towel while the surface is still wet. After wiping, brush a little transparent liquid polymer clay over the area to replace the base coat.

3 Using the template as a guide for your design, draw the point of a skewer or needle tool through the dots of color from the center of the star outward to one of the points.

4 Continue to draw the skewer or needle tool through the dots of color until you've created a pattern that fans out to the points.

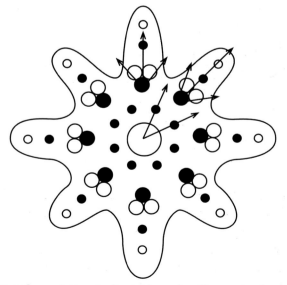

5 Use the template or create your own pattern to decorate the other ornaments. When you are happy with the designs, bake the ornaments again for 20 minutes at 275° F (135° C). (If the transparent liquid polymer clay has filled in the hole, don't worry about it now. You can easily drill through it after the ornament has baked.) If you want to make two-sided ornaments, flip the cooled ornament over, and repeat the process on the other side. Rebaking will not harm the finished side. After you've finished painting and baking, wipe the cooled ornaments with rubbing alcohol to remove any residual oil from the transparent liquid polymer clay or your hands. Use the paintbrush to apply a coat of varnish. After it dries, thread each of the holes with gold cord hangers or ribbon.

Dot the paint as indicated, and pull your tool outward in the direction of the arrows.

Mosaic Face Clock

This clever timepiece makes the phrase "face of the clock" take on new meaning!
See you at half past an eyelash!

Designer: Irene Semanchuk Dean

Photocopies of clock template and numbers template
(page 75)

4 ounces (112 g) of black polymer clay

4 ounces (112 g) of white polymer clay

½ ounce (14 g) gold polymer clay

Gessoed hardboard (such as Masonite), cut to 5½ inches (13.8 cm)
square, with hole drilled in center to accommodate shaft
of clock mechanism

Small paintbrush

Heat-resistant PVA glue

Straightedge or ruler

Pencil

Scissors

Rolling pin or pasta machine

Cutting blade

Craft knife

Plain white paper

Drinking straw

Brayer or rolling pin

Cyanoacrylate glue

Small V-shaped printmaking gouge made for cutting lineoleum
block (found at art supply stores)

Sculpting tool or spoon used only for polymer clay

Small square of stiff plastic (such as a credit card)

Brayer or rolling pin

Baby wipe cloths

Masking tape

400-,. 600-, and 800-grit wet/dry sandpaper

Soft buffing cloth or buffing wheel, optional

1 Use the paintbrush or your fingertips to coat the masonite with a light, even coat of glue, and allow it to dry overnight. Use the pencil and straightedge to draw lines that form a cross on the hardboard square. (You'll use these lines to guide you in placing the clay pieces later.) Cut out the circular clock template.

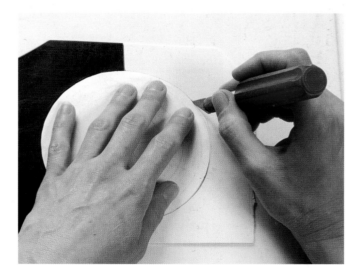

2 Use the rolling pin or pasta machine to roll out the white polymer clay to just under ⅛-inch (3 mm) thickness. The piece should measure at least 6 by 3 inches (15 x 7.5 cm). Repeat this process with the black polymer clay. Place the two sheets on your work surface. Use the straightedge and the cutting blade to trim one 6-inch-long (15 cm) side on each sheet. Butt the two sheets together on white paper. Center the circle template over the seam joining the two pieces of clay. Trace around the template with a craft knife, and mark the center of the circle on the clay. Carefully remove the outer ring of clay, and set it aside intact.

the eye. Use the drinking straw to cut out the pupil from each eye, then swap them. Position each eye in the face.

3 Cut apart the clock template along the lines dividing the parts of the face. Position the nose/forehead template on the circular piece of clay, and cut out around it with the craft knife. Remove the template, and leave the clay intact. Repeat this process with the templates for the lips, eyes, and cheek and forehead triangles.

4 Peel off the pieces for the nose/forehead, lips, and cheek triangles. (To do this with minimal distortion, lift and bend the paper slightly as you do it.) Flip and reposition these pieces as shown. (Note that the forehead triangles at the very top of the face remain in the same position.) Cut out a hole in the center of the face with a drinking straw.

5 Remove the eyes, and position them on your work surface. With the end of your pencil, trace the irises onto the eyes, using the template as a guide. Cut each out with the craft knife, and then reverse the irises in

6 When all the parts of the face are in place on the paper, position the piece of masonite beside it. Move each piece carefully onto the masonite by bending the paper slightly and peeling it off. Use the center hole and the guidelines you drew in step one to assist in repositioning the face. Retrieve the clay that you removed in step 2, and cut it in half from side to side to form two corners of white clay and two of black clay. Frame the face with the clay by placing it on the masonite backing as shown. Gently smooth out any air bubbles.

7 Lay the clock number template from page 75 on top of the face. Use the drinking straw to remove small circles of clay to represent each number. Reposition the circular pieces in the holes so that black is against white and white is against black. Lay a piece of clean white paper over the clock face, and use a rolling pin or brayer to gently rub over the entire face to ensure good adhesion to the masonite and remove air bubbles. Clean away excess clay from the center

hole with the craft knife so that it matches the one in the masonite. Run your cutting blade along the edges of the masonite to remove excess clay from the sides. Bake for 15 minutes at the clay manufacturer's recommended temperature. Allow the clay to cool.

8 Roll out a ⅛-inch-thick (3 mm) sheet of black clay, and cut two strips from it that measure 5½ inches (13.8 cm) by ⅜ inch (9 mm). Repeat this process with white clay. Place a couple of drops of cyanoacrylate glue along the edge of one of the facial quadrants, and push each segment into place to form a frame, as shown. (Note that each strip wraps around a corner.) Bake the piece again for 15 minutes. When the clock has cooled, use the V-shaped gouge to define the lines between the black and white pieces of clay. (See page 52 for tips.) To make smooth lines, hold the lino block

cutter in one place on the clock, and use the other hand to carefully move it under the cutter. Brush away the bits of shaved off clay.

9 Roll the gold clay into long, ⅟₁₆-inch-wide (1.5 mm) pieces. Press these strands into the spaces between the black and white clay. Use a sculpting tool or the back of a spoon to force the gold clay into the spaces. Scrape away the excess gold clay from the surface with a small piece of stiff plastic. When you have grouted all spaces, use a baby wipe cloth to clean all excess grout from the surface. Bake the clock again for 15 minutes. Allow it to cool. Protect the exposed masonite at the center hole with a piece of masking tape, and sand the surface with wet/dry sandpaper. (Wet the sandpaper, not the clock.) Buff the surface if desired, and assemble the clock mechanism in the clock's hole according to the instructions.

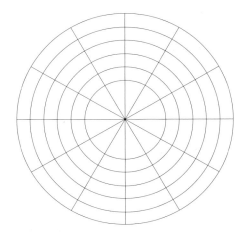

Enlarge 200%

Rhythmic Necklace and Earrings

Repeating elements and abstract shapes are combined to make a stunning jewelry set. If you want to remain unnoticed, leave this set at home! Otherwise, prepare yourself for inquisitive, approving looks.

Designer: Edith Siegel

Photocopy of templates for necklace and earrings (page 78)

4 ounces (112 g) of olive green polymer clay

¼ ounce (7 g) each of silver, gold, and white polymer clay

Rolling pin or pasta machine

Cutting blade

Several sheets of smooth paper

Two 36-inch (.9 m) lengths of ¹⁄₁₆-inch (1.5 mm)-diameter brass rod (available at hardware stores), or 40 quilting pins

Wire cutters or nippers

Hardbacked book or small wooden block

Texturing materials (page 16)

Scissors

Hole punch

Clay gun with discs (available at craft stores)

Needle tool

Beading thread and beading needle

2 clam shell beads

Beading cement

Necklace clasp

Pliers

2 earring jump rings

2 ear wires for earrings

1 Roll out the olive green polymer clay to a ¹⁄₁₆-inch (1.5 mm) thickness. Use the photocopied template for the necklace and the cutting blade to cut out each of the geometric shapes numbered 1 through 19. Place the templates on the green clay, and use the cutting blade to cut out two of each of the shapes to serve as fronts and backs of the necklace pieces. Lay each pair of shapes side by side on a piece of paper.

2 Refer to the templates for the dotted lines on each shape. Use the wire cutters or nippers to cut the brass rod into pieces that fit across and extend beyond the width of each shape along these lines. Position the brass rods. (Note that the wires laid on top of shapes #1 and #19 meet at the top of the bead.) Place a small piece of paper on top of each shape, and gently press the brass rods into the clay by placing a hardbacked book or small wooden block on top. Position each identically shaped piece of clay on top of its corresponding piece, and press the two together in the same manner.

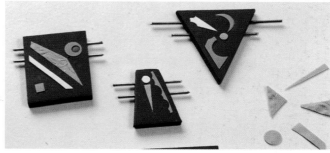

3 Use the rolling pin or pasta machine to roll out paper-thin sheets from the silver, gold, and white clay. Use texturing materials to add texture to the sheets of clay. Bake the sheets for 10 minutes, and remove them from the oven while they're warm. Weigh them down with the stack of books to flatten them. After the sheets are cool, use the scissors or hole punch to cut out decorative motifs. Place these motifs in a pleasing arrangement on the front of every other shape that will make up the finished necklace. Use your fingertips to gently press them into the unbaked clay and embed them slightly. Bake the shapes for 20 minutes according to the clay manufacturer's instructions.

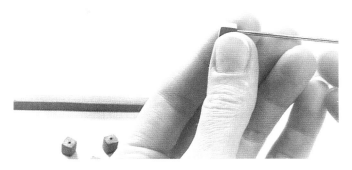

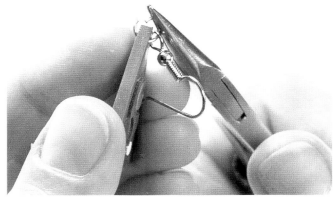

4 To make the squared beads that finish the necklace, use a clay gun fitted with a ³⁄₁₆-inch (5 mm) square-shaped disc to extrude a length of clay that is about 10 inches (25 cm) long. (If you don't use a clay gun, roll a sheet of clay to ³⁄₁₆ inch [5 mm] thick, and cut a strip as wide as it is thick.) Cut this strip into 20 pieces, each about ⅜ inch (9 mm) long, to form the beads. Pierce a hole with the needle tool through each bead to accommodate a double thickness of beading thread later. Bake the beads for 20 minutes.

6 To make the earrings, cut out the triangular shapes. Roll out a sheet of green clay that is approximately ⅛ inch thick. Use the cutting blade to cut out these shapes from the clay. Embellish these with decorative elements as you did the necklace pieces. Use the needle tool to make a hole in the top of each shape, and bake it for 20 minutes. Use pliers to attach a jump ring and an ear wire through the hole in each earring.

5 Sand off any rough edges from the geometric shapes and beads, and buff the surfaces with a soft cloth. Cut two 30-inch (75 cm) pieces of beading thread. Thread one of them into the beading needle. Use the template as a guide to string the geometric shapes and beads onto one of the threads through the top holes. Tie a temporary knot at each end to keep the pieces in place. String the second piece of beading thread through the bottom row of holes. (Both ends of the thread will emerge through a single hole in beads #1 and #19.) When you have strung all the pieces together, string a clam shell bead onto each end. Tie a square knot in each end, and carefully place a dot of beading cement on each knot. Allow it to dry, trim the excess thread with scissors, and close each clam shell bead. Attach the necklace clasp with pliers.

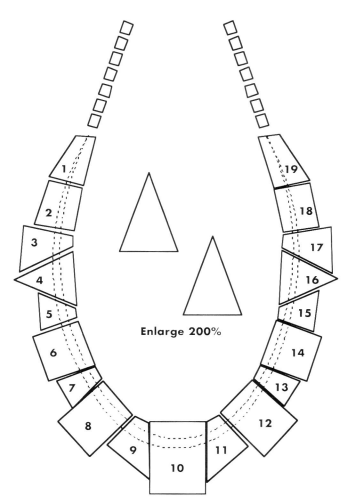

Enlarge 200%

Designers

Jody Bishel has been exploring ways to use Liquid Sculpey with polymer clay since its introduction in 1996. She specializes in organic vessel forms. Her work has been exhibited nationally.

Debbie Krueger is the current President of the Houston Polymer Clay Guild and has been working with polymer clay since 1989. She teaches polymer clay techniques to people of all ages, and sells her work through art shows. She finds inspiration for her work in her surroundings, especially nature.

Heather Tynes Roselli has been working with polymer clay since 1994. She currently sells her work at local arts and crafts shows, retail shops, and at http://members.home.net/claythings. She teaches classes and demonstrates for clay manufacturers at local arts and crafts stores.

Edith Siegel holds a Master's degree in Fine Arts from San Jose State University. During an artistic career of over 20 years, she taught art and craft classes for children and adults, and pursued her major interests in printmaking and ceramics. Shortly after moving to North Carolina she discovered polymer clay, which is now her main focus.

Harriet Smith has been experimenting with polymer clay for three years. She sells her work through small galleries and shops specializing in handmade crafts and at craft shows along the Gulf Coast of the United States. Inspiration often comes from the long walks taken through the parks and funky shops found near her New Orleans home, where the best ideas are often found in the most unexpected places!

Diane Wilson Villano discovered polymer clay in 1995 and co-founded the Southern Connecticut Polymer Clay Guild in 1997. She is currently President of the Guild and finds sharing ideas and techniques with other members one of the most rewarding aspects of working with polymer clay. Her work is displayed and sold at local galleries and art exhibitions.

Top: Irene Semanchuk Dean, Necklace and earring set with mirror image beads

Bottom: Irene Semanchuk Dean, Tiled mirror with canework, faux wood, faux jade, mokume gane, photo transfer, and texturing

Index

Suppliers

for liquid polymer clay and other products:

POLYMER CLAY EXPRESS
25-5 Broad Street PMB 242
Freehold, New Jersey 07728
Toll free: 800-844-0138
Fax: 732-431-2986
E-mail: PolyExp@polymerclayexpress.com
Website: http://www.polymerclayexpress.com

THE CLAY FACTORY OF ESCONDIDO
P. O. Box 460598
Escondido, California 92046-0598
Toll free: 877-728-5739
E-mail: clayfactoryinc@clayfactoryinc.com
website: http://www.clayfactoryinc.com

ZIGZAG POLYMER CLAY SUPPLIES
8 Cherry Place
Casebrook
Christchurch 8005
New Zealand
E-mail: petra@zigzag.co.nz
Website: http://www.zigzag.co.nz/catalogue.html

THE POLYMER CLAY PIT
Meadow Rise, Low Road, Wortham, Diss,
Norfolk IP22 1SQ United Kingdom
Tel: 01379 646019
Fax: 01379 646016
E-mail: claypit@heaser.demon.co.uk
Website: http://www.heaser.demon.co.uk/claypit.htm

PICTURE PERFECT RENDITIONS
340 Walter Drive, Keswick,
Ontario L4P 3A7
Toll free in N. America: 877-811-CLAY
Fax: 905- 476-8161
E-mail: rredmond@interhop.net
website: http://www.geocities.com/Eureka/
        Promenade/1791/index.html

Information Sources

NATIONAL POLYMER CLAY GUILD
Suite 115-345
1350 Beverly Road
McLean, Virginia 22101
website: www.npcg.org
Information: 202-895-5212
Yearly memberships available

IRENE SEMANCHUK DEAN
P.O. Box 1535
Weaverville, North Carolina 28787
E-mail: good.night.irene@pobox.com
Website: www.good-night-irene.com